Did You See That Ghost?

Joe Sledge

Books by Joe Sledge

Did You See That? A GPS Guide to North Carolina's
Out of the Ordinary Attractions

Did You See That? On The Outer Banks

Did You See That, Too?

Did You See That Ghost?

A Ghostly Guide to the Haunts
Of the Old North State

Joe Sledge

For John, who loves a ghost story as much as me.
Maybe more.

Table of Contents

Introduction

It wasn't a crackling campfire for me; it was a creaking rocking chair on the front porch of my beach house where I first heard the scary tales of the ghosts of North Carolina. I grew up on rich legends of the coast, replete with bloodthirsty pirates and spectral sailors. Why, I was sure I saw pirates burying treasure late at night right on the beach by my house. Just as sure as I was that I saw a floating red light over the far distant sand dunes every evening when the sun went down. Those things that go bump in the night? Well, that was probably just my oldest brother John thumping on the underside of the beach house when the rest of us went to bed.

I mean, it was him, wasn't it?

North Carolina is truly a haunted land. The tales of ghosts and legends have been told well, whether on a front porch, by a campfire, or by storytellers like Charles Harry Whedbee or Nancy Roberts, both of whom penned some of the greatest collections of ghostly tales about the Old North State. There are just so many strange haunts and even just weird events across the state.

When I started this, I knew I would find a lot of legends, some haunting, and a few of those "Dude, no, really!" stories of a local urban legend. I was surprised to discover so much more. The legends are great. With so much history in the state, it's not surprising that there are a lot of legends to be told. Blackbeard haunts the coast, battles fought long ago still leave their mark upon the land, and so many people either lost their lives tragically or were so content in their home that they never left this world. I also liked all the haunted bridges, all the ghosts that pop up on a dark night in stories meant to scare kids or give teenagers an excuse to be out late.

One thing I wasn't sure of was if I believed them. In the beginning, I leaned more toward the non believer rather than just a skeptic. I love the legends, but ghosts, real ghosts? I didn't buy it. I respected others opinions on it, but I just couldn't buy into it myself.

Now, well, I just don't know. I mean, some of the stories don't add up, but at the same time, there are a lot of people who may have seen or felt *something* that I'm not going to poo-poo the idea. Which I think is fair. Ghosts may seem unlikely to me, but I'll give them a chance, especially if they are burying pirate gold in my beach.

I want to add this little aside to my readers, especially parents. Now, I loved the old ghost story books I read as a kid. But still, they creeped me out. All those eerie double exposure photos and hair-raising stories... Ghost tales usually involve a sad or tragic death, and no matter what, the idea of a ghost can tax a young mind. My other books were fairly family friendly, and as much as I tried to keep this accessible, there is no hiding the rather sanguine details of many of these stories. I'm not saying none of these stories are for kids. I think I just mean, that, as a parent, do your job. Don't tell your kids the tales that will keep them up at night or give them nightmares. Explain the difference between a campfire tale and a legend. Look at the history. Make them curious, not scared.

And for everyone, I hope you enjoy this book. A lot of places in here are great to visit. Some are not so great. They are haunted, after all. Get out, have fun, be careful, stay safe. Don't get slimed.

-*Joe Sledge*

Reference

Rather than use my usual rating of oddity and difficulty, I chose to use a set of icons to represent the different types of hauntings in the book. While not inclusive, they will give the reader a good idea of what type of ghost story they are dealing with.

Historical The ghost story exists mostly in history, and there may be little to no current evidence of any haunting or event. These stories are tied in with famous events in the state's history.

No Trespassing The area the ghost appears is off limits, or just inaccessible. It may not be dangerous, but visiting is not allowed, or you can't get there.

Dangerous Different than No Trespassing, this place is accessible, but you still shouldn't go. Well, you should never go anywhere without permission, but these are best seen from afar.

Happy The ghost tales show a benevolent or not so dangerous spirit. The place will be pretty nice to visit, too.

Spooky Ghost stories are scary, but these spots will just make it worse, especially at night. You can try whistling through that graveyard, but it just makes it easier for the ghosts to find you.

Scientific There's probably a logical reason for the story. But who wants to ruin a good story with facts?!

Urban Legend "Dude! No, really! I was there!" Yeah, it's a great tale, but it was probably made up to scare middle school kids.

Northern Coast

Currituck Light Keepers House

Corolla   36.37660° -75.83125°

For centuries the barrier islands of the Outer Banks have been a harsh realm of windswept land, ruled by the ancient gods of wind and ocean. The shores, land, and trees all bowed to the ever present forces of nature. All creatures that lived there seemed to do so only through subsistence, a battle to survive more than to thrive on the barren coast.

Even some of the first people who were brought to the Outer Banks came by tragedy or accident. Many early residents were stranded on the shore by a shipwreck. The colony of Wash Woods, near present day Corolla, that straddled the border of North Carolina and Virginia was founded by shipwrecked sailors and passengers from an early expedition toward Cape Henry. The North Carolina coast may not have been where they wanted to end up, but the colonists made do with the location that they were handed. The soft fertile soil of the sound side where the overwash from the ocean had deposited its soft loam became farmland, and wild food was plentiful. Fish and game quickly became a staple, and would remain important for years along the northern coast, with hunting lodges springing up along the Currituck coast.

What lead to the shipwrecks along the coast also lead to the prevention of them. The dangerous coast that would be known as the Graveyard of the Atlantic would quickly become dotted with lighthouses to mark the shore, from Bald Head Island, Cape Lookout, Cape Hatteras, and up to Bodie Island. However, the stretch between Cape Henry and Bodie Island would remain a darkened mystery. It would be especially risky for southbound sailing ships, trying to hug the coast to avoid the Gulf Stream and its relentless northward push.

In 1872 the Currituck lighthouse would be built. The natural red brick sentinel would stand watch with a warning eye out to all ships at sea, to tell them to beware the coastline.

The ocean would be unforgiving to the people on the shore as well as to seagoing craft. Locals to the coast knew to respect the waves, and never turned their back on the sea. Keepers of the light would know the dangers the ocean posed, considering the job they held. Unfortunately, what might be clear to an adult could seem muddled to a child.

Sadie Johnson was the adopted daughter of Garner George Johnson and his wife Lucy. After her parents died, little Sadie was adopted by the assistant keeper Johnson, and lived with them while he served at Currituck Beach Lighthouse. Sadie embraced the isolation and wilderness that was the Corolla coast of the early 1900s, particularly the open windswept beaches along the oceanside. She would wander off to the shore to play in the sand, building castles and scolding the unrelenting waves when they invariably washed the palaces down. Locals would warn the girl not to turn her back on the sea. The ocean was wild and no human could hold back the tide, the locals knew. But Sadie would continue to go to the shore and play. Until the ocean finally took her from the sand.

Sadie was washed out to sea. She went missing for a day, until local fishermen found her lifeless body the next morning, washed up miles to the north. Heartbroken, her family would have the little girl's wake in the north room of the keepers' quarters, Sadie's bedroom.

Sadie's death would not be the only tragedy to grace the lighthouse's quarters. The North Room would also be tied to other mysterious and tragic deaths. A guest of a keeper, visiting from the mainland, would reside in the North Room on her trip, only to become sick and die.

A more morbid story would also become attached to the north room. An unnamed keeper's wife would come down with tuberculosis, a dreaded and deadly disease of the time. Forced into isolation in the North Room, she would slowly wither away the days while the rest of the families would go on with their lives. She would sit observing them while she stayed alone in the north room. The disease would ultimately take her life. So feared was tuberculosis that all her clothing was packed away in a barrel and sealed. The barrel would stay in the north room long after the lighthouse would become automated and the keeper's quarters abandoned.

The hearty locals of the area knew of the woman's death, and of the dreaded barrel still inside the darkened and decrepit home. They warned their children to stay away, to keep out of the house, and especially from that barrel, full of disease from the old lady's garments. Kids being kids, they immediately went to the old house and cracked open the barrel, removing all the clothes and playing a macabre game of dress up in the cold, salty manor. Children danced like adults, ghosts long gone come back to flesh and bone in the

house that had kept the keepers safe for decades. When the distraught and furious parents found out, the children were soundly punished and the clothes gathered with the barrel staves and burned to ash in the yard by the light.

So with all the death and sadness that accompanied the north room of the quarters, it is no wonder there is a haunting attached to it. When the quarters were finally reopened for refurbishment and tours, workers and visitors alike felt a strangeness about the room. Carpenters working on the restoration who knew nothing of its history would comment on how they could not stay in the north room, as it filled them with dread to remain for long. And when visitors would tour the site, several people would comment on the mysterious feeling they would get, some refusing to set foot into the room, such was their apprehension.

Today, the keeper's quarters are well kept as part of the lighthouse grounds, managed by Outer Banks Conservationists, a nonprofit started when the lighthouse and quarters were in desperate need of repair and no one was willing to conserve the historical properties. The lighthouse and third assistant keeper's quarters are open for visiting, but the main building is used as a private residence for current keepers of the light as well as guests who are working on other historical studies such as shipwrecks in the area. The quarters and the north room are not available to visit from the inside, though they can be seen from outside when visiting the lighthouse grounds.

Corolla Hunt Club

Corolla   36.37331° -75.83230°

The cold salt air that blows off of the Atlantic Ocean in the winter may feel like a bitter knife to many a visitor to the northern Outer Banks, but decades ago, the quiet village of Corolla would have been a welcome respite to wealthy visitors from up north in cold New England. To them, January on the North Carolina coast was more like a nice spring day.

Mild temperatures and the peaceful isolation drove rich outdoorsmen to come to Corolla with the promise of wild game in abundance. The Atlantic Flyway brought ducks and geese by the thousands, and hunters easily could shoot to their hearts' content, returning to a rustic but warm hunt club with a plan to go out later for fishing, or simply sit by a roaring fire and wait for another sunrise.

And that's what happened for Edward Collins Knight, Jr. and his wife Marie Louise Lebel. Knight, an industrialist from Rhode Island, and his wife, bought a nice but average hunt club, the Lighthouse Club, and turned it into a private residence for themselves and their friends, renaming it Corolla Island. The building would be grandiose, with hot and cold running water, oil heat, a swimming pool, and decorated with a floor to ceiling pink tile kitchen, Tiffany lamps, and ornate furniture. The building was completed in 1925. The Knights and guests would come down every October to stay the winter, leaving only when the promise of spring in Rhode Island was fulfilled.

That is, they did so until 1933. For several years, the Knights would enjoy their coastal retreat, a salt air Xanadu that was shared by few. Marie would hunt, a pastime not allowed to women in the other hunt clubs, as well as drink, and chase off local dogs with a small revolver she carried in her purse. Edward would hunt as well, then retire to the warmth of his study to enjoy a cigar. Life was good for the wealthy couple. In 1933, they would come to their club in October, as they always did. But instead of staying through the winter, they would only remain three weeks before packing and leaving abruptly for their cold Rhode Island home. The couple would never return, dying in 1936 without ever visiting Corolla, their winter home, ever again. The Knights would never speak of why they left, nor why they would not go back.

One thing is for sure, though. In the decades since, the building that would become the Whalehead Club would stir up abundant tales of ghosts, haunts, and spirits to walk the halls and frequent the dark corners of the old hunt club. In the 1960s, a security guard stayed in the darkened house while a hurricane raged outside. Alone but for his dog, the man's pet suddenly began snarling, barking, whimpering at a dark corner of Mrs. Knight's room near the stairs. While he could see nothing, the dog would not be sated, his aggression and fear so real at the shadowy threat. Rather than stay and face the unknown, the man and dog left into the heart of the storm.

A couple later stayed in the same room, Mrs. Knight's bedroom, when in the middle of the night the husband awoke to a creaking bathroom door, swaying in the breeze through the open windows. After visiting the bathroom, with the intent to brace the door to stop the creaking, the man found his wife already at the job, kneeling at the base of the door as if to drive a wedge under it, so the husband stepped carefully around her. Climbing into bed, he was surprised to find his wife already there, still sound asleep.

The Whalehead Club has more than a normal share of haunted events. Volunteers to the home have heard pots and pans banging around in an empty kitchen, an elevator operating that should have been locked down, and footsteps heard in an empty hallway. Guests on tours have seen men talking in a corner of a room, only to have them vanish when other people go looking for the gentlemen. Edward Knight's study can occasionally be filled with the scent of good cigars, a popular pastime of the man when he relaxed in his private room.

Perhaps most frightening are the apparitions in the basement, where much of the ghostly appearances seem to happen. Footsteps from no human tread have been heard as people walk out of the basement, lights appear on security cameras in the darkened room, and most frightening is the appearance of a little girl in the subterranean vault. On a tour a little boy was frightened to the point of crying when a ghostly girl reached out to grab him, reaching, but not quite getting to him. Others have heard her call out, asking to play. The ethereal child seems to only reside in the darkness of the basement, never finding her way out, never up to the levels of the living, always below, waiting.

The Whalehead Club has opened its doors to numerous paranormal investigations, and the ghost hunters find the place to be extremely active. So popular are the ghost tales that the Whalehead Club offers evening tours telling of the haunted history of the place. Visitors can take a daylight ghost tour, or for a more moody tour, take the nighttime Legends, Lore, and Ghost Tour done every Wednesday evening during the summer. But if you hear footsteps behind you, just keep walking.

Ghost of the Black Pelican

Kitty Hawk   36.06706° -75.69077°

In the late 1800s people rarely chose to live on the Outer Banks. The islands were mostly barren, with loping dunes and wind twisted yaupon being the few graces to an otherwise empty landscape. Visitors were rarer still, and most were not there by choice. The churning Atlantic would easily hide a sandbar or beach from the ships that sailed or steamed by, causing a wreck, where, if they were lucky, the sailors would be rescued and stranded upon the coastline of Kitty Hawk.

So it was without a doubt that most of the people who were there were hearty indeed, rough hewn men who squared themselves to the biting salty brine that threw itself against the coast. The toughest and bravest of them would have been the men of the life saving stations that dotted the empty coast. While the families that lived on the Outer Banks nestled themselves  into warm soundside cottage homes, these men stood watch over the rain and storm that might throw a ship into the clutches of a fickle sea. This was the setting for the Kitty Hawk Lifesaving Station in 1884.

Keeper James Hobbs ran a crew of six surfmen, each ready and willing at any time to do their duty to save the lives of stranded sailors and passengers on their stretch of beach. Hobbs ran his crew rough, but the men responded well, liking the demand and attention, delivering more than asked. They supported and counted on each other, never wanting to be the one to let another down in time of crisis.

But there was someone who was jealous of James Hobbs' success. Theopolis "T.L." Daniels had an intense hatred of Hobbs, perhaps envious of the keeper's popularity or desirous of his job. Daniels took every opportunity to insult or provoke the man, trying to rile Hobbs into an act of violence. Daniels would often find a way to attack Hobbs' wife, even going so far as to spit tobacco juice on her dress. To say the two disliked each other would be a gross understatement.

In July, Daniels had been able to bring forth an inspector to judge Hobbs, accusing him of using government paint on his own personal boat. At the inquisition, the anger between the two was palpable. Daniels tried to provoke Hobbs by saying, "If you so much as draw a pen knife on me, I'll kill you!" Hobbs responded that he was unarmed, and that Daniels merely wanted an excuse to use a pistol he had concealed. Daniels stood up to draw on Hobbs, his anger brought to a pique. While he struggled to clear the pistol from his jacket, the rest of the sailors in the room left in haste, fearing the upcoming bloodbath would take them, too. Hobbs, who had faced danger head on, reached into a nearby closet and removed a loaded shotgun. The investigator, a Lt. E.C. Clayton, was caught in the middle, but Hobbs simply lowered the shotgun over Clayton's shoulder and blasted Daniels. The shot went through Daniels' shoulder, knocking him to the floor. Daniels attempted to rise and cock his pistol at the menacing Hobbs, but Hobbs let loose with the other barrel, killing his bitter rival in the floor of the station.

While the rest of the crew, and Lt. Clayton especially, were aghast at the bloody violence, they knew that Daniels not only had it coming when he tried to draw upon Hobbs, but the mean old man would leave the earth no poorer for his loss. Gathering up the sanguine remains, the crew that normally would do life saving performed a more somber act by taking Daniels out and dumping his body into the ocean.

Fast forward to 1993, when the remains of the old life saving station itself would be saved from the sea. The building, already moved twice to pull it back from the ocean, crossed the beach road and was turned into the Black Pelican. The gingerbread design of the old station can still be seen along the roofline, but the more permanent record of the lifesaving station may be of a more spectral nature.

T.L. Daniels' ghost is still around.

Near the front of the restaurant, a dark stain has marred the wooden floor, right where Daniels fell and bled out. This physical reminder is not the only remnant of Daniels' death, though. Workers have heard footsteps late at night, the heavy trod of a man pacing the upstairs of the restaurant. Other noises, rattling, objects moving, are not uncommon. Doors have shut on their own, with a hard slam that sets a heart to pounding. The stairway to the upstairs is known to have a cold spot, a gloomy cast of dread that will cut through someone when they pass by. But most frightening of all are the strange manifestations that people have seen. There is more than one time a drink glass or plate has skidded from a table to the floor. More frightening would be the times people have actually seen a figure in the restaurant. A haunting apparition has been spotted hovering in the corner late after closing by an employee. And the ghost has been seen in other sections of the restaurant, even in the bathroom, which has been a terrifying sight to someone who thinks they are alone in there.

Since T.L. Daniels is the most prominent death in the building, especially when the building was made to save lives, it is thought that he still haunts the place. It could be that between his traumatic death, and his bloodthirsty desire, his spirit still resides in the building. Now with no others to fight, he wants to do the job he longed for so much he would kill, and ultimately die for. But with the lifesaving station now a happy restaurant, he cannot rest in peace, for the job of keeper is long gone. He is forced to watch, day after day, a restless soul who will not be satisfied.

The Ghost Light of Run Hill

A Spooky Side Trip

When I was a little kid, we would spend our summers at our beach house in Kill Devil Hills, a move of only a few miles from our soundside home. It was a wonderful old place, with screened in porches, open windows with big shutters to shield us from the heat of the day. Salt and sand covered everything, which was just fine for us kids. The house was always filled with family and friends. Brothers, cousins, aunts and uncles, grandparents, the place was scattered with them. We had family like other houses had mice. As the youngest, I was forced to sleep upon the sofa in the living room, with the small consolation of being the first one up for cereal in the morning.

But my favorite thing was to sit on the front porch in a rocking chair and watch the evening slip away. Back then, with few houses along the island, you could see all the way to the other side, to a white sand dune that shielded Nags Head Woods from the winter winds. Run Hill was a vibrant spot, full of persimmon trees and yaupon, a place for people to take their four wheel drives and party into the night. But my brothers told me of another more sinister part of the hill.

The ghost light.

I saw it a few times. It was a strange red light, a single one, not a headlight or anything like that. Brighter than a star, it just hovered there, maybe ten feet above the sand. It never moved. When the sun would set, it would finally fade out to nothing, leaving me to wonder if I ever really saw it at all.

Being a little kid, I neither had the wherewithal nor the fortitude to go and investigate the light. There seemed to be no legend attached to the thing. It just was a strange light that appeared. Sadly, with the buildup of homes and businesses, along with taller trees, I lost sight of the dunes over the years. The dunes are now protected, part of a state natural area that still blocks the salt winds from the tiny ecosystem of Nags Head Woods. Which is a good thing, because Nags Head Woods has its own spooky stories to tell.

Nags Head Woods

Kill Devil Hills   35.9898° -75.66455°

It would be hard to hide in the shadows when there is nothing but open sand and bright sun on the coast of North Carolina. Luckily for the spooks and demons of the coast, there is Nags Head Woods, a lush overgrown maritime forest that holds more than its share of secrets. The tree filled preserve is full of paths and sand roads, along with overgrown old houses and requisite graveyards of people long passed. With only minimum care, trees grow into the graves. It is said that if you tickle a tree in the graveyards of Nags Head Woods, the corpse will laugh and shake the limbs.

The old forest has long been a setting for spooky or nefarious deeds. The dark canopy of trees and twisty, empty road lend themselves to tales of the macabre. In the 1970s it was evil secret societies, the 80s brought tales of demons and devils, the 90s were stories of witchcraft, and so on, forever ending with the conclusive "Oh, yeah, it's true..."

If that wasn't enough, a Goat Man legend was spawned in the woods. The Goat Man isn't specific to the Outer Banks; there seem to be several of them. What makes this legend different is that most stories create a strange horned human goat monster, this was just the name attributed to a crazy man who lived alone in the woods, often found terrorizing the local teenagers. He lived in a small cabin, a yellow house nestled into the woods, and performed horrific rituals to animals. People still tell of how Goat Man lives there, even long after the building being abandoned.

Nags Head Woods is a preserve now, and maintained in a beautiful organic state. Visitors are usually monitored, and it really isn't a good place to visit at night.

Unpainted Aristocracy

Nags Head 35.95717° -75.62403°

Today it may seem odd to think of the beach at Nags Head to be an inhospitable place, but in the 1800s, most people preferred the calm safety of soundside living. Even if the life they lead was poor, at least they were protected from the fickle tendencies of a sometimes calm, sometimes raging Atlantic. In Nags Head, most people lived in simple homes just south of Jockey's Ridge, where the boats from Roanoke Island and the mainland would put in. Legends held that the early residents were descendents of Breakers, land pirates that would lure unsuspecting ships into the shallows in the night, then board them and kill the crew, taking whatever was valuable or useful.

It wasn't until 1855 when Dr. W. G. Pool, a doctor from Elizabeth City, built the first beach house on the coast. In order to keep his wife from being lonely, he bought several parcels and sold them to his friends for the hefty sum of $1 each. The houses were made of whatever was available. Scrap lumber and shipwrecks could be included in the houses. Since paint was an unnecessary extravagance, the homes were not painted, except for the occasional splash on a shutter. The rich families that would come down to escape the hot still summers inland gave name to their cottages, the Unpainted Aristocracy.

With the houses being so old, and there being so many of them, ghost stories abound in the area, in and around the homes. Legends tell of shadow people who walk the coast, or sit on the porches of the old houses. Theories of their history include the spirits of both the pirates and the victims lost at sea, as well as former residents of the old homes.

One of the houses definitely has a spectral presence. A ghostly figure, dark, opaque, without any detail, haunts the downstairs kitchen and living room of one of the private homes on the shore. It has been spotted occasionally by the owners and guests, who don't really like to discuss their permanent guest. The kitchen door will creak, just a little, only enough to get a sideways glance, and there it will be, in the doorway. The ghost moves off if anyone looks at it.

Considering the number of old houses on the beach, there probably are more stories like this. Most are privately owned, though some can be rented. A shadowy figure may or may not be included in the stay. If you find a treasure chest buried in the sand, be sure to leave some of that gold for whoever buried it. They may still be looking.

Ghost of the Roanoke Island Inn

Manteo   35.90779° -75.67035°

There are scary ghosts and mischievous ghosts, benevolent and malevolent, but the Roanoke Island Inn actually has an embarrassed ghost.

The Roanoke Island Inn sits across from the peaceful waters of Shallowbag Bay. The house has stood since the 1860s, first as a home, and later as an inn. It has been kept in the family, as descendants of the builders, Asa and Martha Jones, still run the place. One descendant was so ashamed of his lot in life that he never left. Not even in death.

Roscoe Jones was a postmaster in Manteo, an honorable and popular job in the town. Unfortunately, Jones was let go of his position, and in his shame, he hid himself away in his house. He would spend the entire day locked in his room, and only leave late at night to come downstairs to get dinner when no one else was around to see him. It would not take long for the man to wither and die, but his spirit would not pass on.

Soon after his death, guests would spot a man in a blue postman's uniform, either walking up the stairs, or leaving the inn. His spirit wanted so bad to still be doing a job that he remained, or at least his pride did.

In addition to the spectral appearances, the inn also has other occurrences typical to a haunting. Footsteps from an empty room, items moving or breaking, even a famous tale of a radio that would not turn off even when unplugged are part of the lore.

A visit to the inn is a worthwhile respite, and if the guest spots a ghost, well, that's just an extra amenity that most hotels don't have. The Roanoke Island Inn is open from Easter to the middle of November.

Gray Man of Hatteras

Buxton   35.25488° -75.5207°

The wind off the coast of Cape Hatteras puffs through white sheets hung on a line stretched over the soft yellow sand that makes up the quiet Buxton beach. A mother absentmindedly watches her two children as they play in the sand by her house on the shore. She goes about her work without thought, following a rhythm draping the sheets and pillowcases over the line, then pinning them down. The sun will dry them quickly, but nothing will stop the permeated salt air from adding the scent of the beach to her linens. The first winds of a storm far off to sea are just rolling in from the south. The warm tropical air brings new scents to the coast. But the storm is long off, she figures. It's more likely to hit farther south, down toward Emerald Isle or Wrightsville Beach. She has no TV, and counts on a static filled radio to get what little information she hears about the storm. There will be plenty of time to get the linens in if the storm ever moves northward. Plenty of time to leave.

Out onto the beach, her husband fishes in the surf. Alone, he casts and reels his line, again, and again, following his own rhythm. The waves roll, but aren't yet stirred to the froth that a hurricane would bring. One more day of fishing, at least, thinks the man. And one more good day alone. He shares the beach with no one, no other pole all the way down to the big Cape Hatteras light, its black and white candy stripe paint scheme bright in the light of day. The light will cut through the night, and the clouds to come, but not now. The sun shines, the breeze blows, and today all is right.

The man can feel the waves washing the shore, and he can feel that something has changed in the wind. He looks down the coastline. In the salt air another man walks up the shore. He is indistinct; a strange haze blurs the man. Dressed all in gray, he seems to be a sailor from a bygone time. He seems to communicate with the fisherman, but no sound comes from the spectral sailor's mouth. If he even has a mouth. The fisherman stops, unafraid of what is happening. On the contrary, he starts to walk closer to the gray sailor. With every step, the ghostly mariner becomes more faint and misty. Before he can get close enough to see a detail on the ghost, the gray man disappears into the salty air.

With that, the wind turns, and the sky begins to turn cloudy. The first true winds of a hurricane reach the coast of Cape Hatteras. Still far off, the storm has changed. It has grown and turned northeast. It will aim for the exposed point of the cape, crossing over and bringing with it wind and rain, as well as a storm surge that will pound into the shore, beating down the dunes in an attempt to get to the beach houses beyond. The man knows what to do.

He runs up the beach, toward his house, his wife and kids still outside. Up the dune, he tells them to come inside, that they must leave, a hurricane is coming, and coming now. The mother leaves her basket on the back porch. The linens still hang on the line. They don't bother packing much, just a change of clothes, and water for the drive. That's it. In their car, they drive away, up Highway 12, turning toward Roanoke Island and the protection of the mainland farther inland. Two and a half hours later, they stop at a motel, a simple drive up room where the kids squeal as they jump on the firm bed and beg for a quarter for the magic fingers machine to shake them while they laugh. The father watches the TV as the reports of the storm roll in. It looks like it is headed toward Hatteras, possibly passing over tiny Ocracoke Island before going north over the sound, the worst path it could take. The mother comes in, a bucket of ice in her arm, two bottles of soda dangling in her fingers. They will ride out the next two nights there as the hurricane passes over their home at the beach.

The family will return to the beach, knowing full well the effects a hurricane can have on a coastal home. Shutters down, windows broken, sand filling the porches, roofs damaged. Those will be the lucky ones. Other houses will be blown down, pulled off the pilings or simply snatched away by the ocean.

But their house, incredibly, is fine. The driveway is clear of sand and debris. The shutters still overhang the windows, screens still in place. No sand on the porch, no sand on the sun deck. Remarkably, her basket is still there, her sheets still hang on the clotheslines.

The family is the recipient of the grace of the Gray Man of Hatteras.

The Gray Man is a ghostly apparition that appears soon before a major hurricane hits the coast of Cape Hatteras. The legend tells that he is the ghost of a sailor who was lost in a shipwreck in a storm at the Cape. So traumatic was the storm that even in death, the sailor still walks the coast, guarding the denizens of the shore from the deadly effects of a hurricane. He approaches as only a ghostly specter. A gray cloud of a man, he usually speaks without sound to the person he finds to warn. The people who see him are not afraid, but actually feel a sense of compassion. When approached, the Gray Man disappears. Some people even think the Gray Man is only a power of nature that is not understood. But anyone who sees him is both given a warning, and a promise. The warning is of an impending storm, one that will be exceptionally bad. Whoever sees the Gray Man should heed this warning and leave immediately. Do not bother to board up the house, do not put away any valuables, don't do anything but leave as soon as possible. In return, the Gray Man protects the house from harm. People who have seen the Gray Man report that while other houses are damaged, theirs is still as they left it. Windows and shingles are still intact. There is no sand blown up against the house. The legend even tells that clothes left out, hanging on the line or draped out to dry will still be there, with no ill effect from the wind.

The Gray Man has been seen several times, at least since the 1940s. So visitors and locals alike should take heed. If a hazy gray clad sailor warns them of an upcoming storm, no matter what the weather stations say, get in the car and go. Nothing of this earth can hold back a hurricane. But just maybe the Gray Man can.

Cape Hatteras Lighthouse

Cape Hatteras   35.25059° -75.52882°

Lighthouses are supposed to be beacons of warning. Their beam shines out from a tall tower far out to sea, flashing a code to mariners at night, warning them of the dangerous shoals close to land. Cape Hatteras Light is especially watchful. The tallest brick lighthouse in the U.S. casts its light out 24 nautical miles to warn off ships from the swirling water and changing shoals that became known as The Graveyard of the Atlantic. So it may seem odd that the lighthouse attracts ghosts and spirits to its light.

While the beach nearby is home to the Gray Man of Hatteras, the light has a multitude of supernatural apparitions. Often seen at the old, original location for the tower, near the shore, were shadowy figures that walked the sand, and climbed the tower. The ghosts were seen often, out of the corner of an unsuspecting visitor's eye, at night or dusk. They are thought to be the last vestiges of a ship's crew, lost on the shoals in a shipwreck. They have appeared around the lighthouse, and in the spiral staircase inside the light.

Another ghost is the figure of a man in a yellow raincoat, like the bright slickers men would wear during rainstorms in an attempt to stay partly dry during the violent storms on the Cape. Some suspect him to be a former keeper. He has, for reasons unknown, been given the name Bob.

But most intriguing is the appearance of a large black and white cat. The big feline, some say it is between 20 and 25 pounds, will come up to visitors to the light and even rub up against their legs. Only when they reach down to pet it or pick the cat up does it vanish. It may be a ghostly pet of a former keeper of the lighthouse, a mouser meant to keep the rodent population down, and the fat kitty just decided to stick around, its job was so satisfying.

Cats seem to play a prominent part of Hatteras lore. The nearby Cora Tree, a place where a mystical witch and her baby were nearly burned to death, holds the legend that the child turned into a giant hissing cat, before both disappeared into a clap of thunder and lightning, splitting the tree. And more earthly feral felines will spend the day at the Red & White Supermarket in Hatteras. Cats are known to gather anywhere they can get scraps, near the grocery store where they are fed by a friendly local, or under the nearby fishing docks, begging for fish. These cats are different, however, in that they are polydactyl, having six toes on a paw. The cats' common ancestor came to Hatteras on a shipwrecked ghost ship, and its descendants have made a home there ever since.

So check those paws before you try to pet a kitty in Hatteras. A ghost cat may disappear before you can pick it up, but a real one can give you a serious scratch.

The Flaming Ship of Ocracoke

Ocracoke   35.181° -75.78362°

It is late at night on September 18, and the sky above Ocracoke is dark as pitch. What little light from the village has long since vanished as most of the islanders have gone to bed. One young boy sits on the beach, and waits. It starts as an orange glow in the water, silently boiling its way out. Along the horizon, it skims across the calm water of the Atlantic. A ship sails in the darkness, but is brightened by the now yellow haze around it. It is an old ship, under power only by sails, sails which bizarrely seem to be burning, but not consumed. A windless night takes the ship across the waters, toward the inlet; the flames never destroy the boat, but just seem to wisp away into ash. The ship disappears before making the safe passage into the protection of the sound. The young boy, alone on the again darkened beach, has witnessed the flaming ship of Ocracoke.

The legend of the Flaming Ship goes back to a gruesome tale from 1710. At the time, the Palatine region of Europe, part of Germany and Switzerland, was under siege of decades of war, and many refugees left to the relative safety of England. The overflow of unskilled labor drove one group, funded by a Swiss baron by the name of Cristoph von Graffnreid, to sail to the New World, to settle in the town of New Bern, a Swiss settlement named after Bern, Switzerland. The group chartered a sailboat to take them there, and packed all their belongings, including chests of valuables, in order to settle in the new land.

Unfortunately for the settlers, the captain and his crew were unscrupulous to say the least. They heard the passengers discussing their valuable cache, and decided to separate the Palatines from their fortune. Arriving at the coast of Ocracoke, the crew waved away the approaching boats meant to shuttle the people first to land, and then to other craft to finish the inland trip up the sounds to New Bern. The captain told his passengers that they would remain onboard for the night, and then go ashore in the morning.

That night, the crew would turn the peaceful hold of sleeping Palatines into a bloody abattoir, killing every man, woman, and child in the silence of the night. After their horrible deed, the crew loaded their long boat with the treasure. After they were finished, the dastardly party then set the ship on fire, and rowed away in the middle of the night toward the safety of the soft white sand beach of Ocracoke.

Amazingly, the crew saw the ship aflame, but not consumed. The sails filled with wind, and slowly at first, began overtaking the now panicked crew in the long boat. They tried to maneuver, but the ship chased them down. The sails burned bright, and the wind swirled the flames. The entire ship glowed a bright orange. It increased speed as it came upon the horrified crew. As it got close, they could hear the moans and cries of the stricken passengers, the tortured souls who had come so far to escape the horrors of war, to be so close, then turned away, left to burn in the hold of a ship.

The ship rammed the little boat, splitting it and upending the crew. Laden as they were, and in the dark, most sank to the bottom of the sea, a final watery grave that was probably still too good for the piratical men. Others floundered in the waves, only to be crushed by the barnacle laden hull, as if the ship itself attempted to scrape away the sin of their act. Only two sailors made it to shore. Locals arrived to find the sailors waterlogged and in fear of their lives. The men confessed their sins, but the haunting of the sailing ship stayed with them the rest of their short lives. The sailors were cursed with the memories of what they had done, and what had then happened to them.

The ship, after delivering its otherworldly revenge, sailed on. It sailed north toward the point of Ocracoke before disappearing into the black of night.

Now, on the first full moon of September, late at night, the ship sails again. From the northern point of the island, the ship will sail in from the Atlantic. Its sails will be unfurled, taught with the wind that pushes it, flaming sheets held fast by flaming ropes. The deck will glow hot with the embers of wood, and if the night is quiet, the mournful sounds of the Palatines will be heard across the ocean. The ship sails on, hoping to pass through the inlet and go onward to New Bern. The passengers are still trying to get to the home they were promised and denied centuries ago. Always still trying, and the ship blinks out every night, cursed to try again the next year, and the year after that, and the year after, forever sailing, never finding its port.

The Flaming Ship of Ocracoke can be seen, if it is sailing, on the new moon of September, a dark night in a dark patch of beach. The ferry runs only into the night, but not overnight, and anyone searching for the ship will need to plan on spending the night on the island. September is a wonderful, quiet time on the coast, but it can also be a time for storms and hurricanes, which brings its own form of pirates and destruction.

Teach's Light

Ocracoke   35.1055° -75.98855°

O cracoke is full of ghosts. You can't swing a boat oar without splashing into some sort of ectoplasmic residue on the island. They walk the homes and inns. The rise up or reach out from graves. Late at night, when the roads are quiet, empty, and dark, they walk the lonely streets of the village. The stories and the people are known to the locals, who recognize family members in the tales. The most famous ghost, however, wasn't a resident. He was not even a welcome guest.

Edward Teach, who was also known as Blackbeard the pirate, lost his life, and his head, in the waters off of Ocracoke. Shot and stabbed by Lt. Maynard and his crew as the dreaded buccaneer fought to the last onboard Maynard's bloodied sloop. As proof of the deed, Blackbeard's head was severed off of his body and hung from the bowsprit of Maynard's boat. The body, and those of Blackbeard's crew, were either dumped over the side or buried in an unmarked mass grave.

For the next 300 years, Blackbeard would find it hard to leave the shore. Locals would see his ghost, a vaporous form without a head, walking the shoreline, or a shadowy figure stalking the woods of Springer Point. The figure exudes a certain vehemence, an evil air about him that creates a feeling of dread, and no one has dared to approach it. Supposedly, Blackbeard is still searching for his head so that he can continue his pirating ways.

Teach's Point is not the only spot that is haunted in Ocracoke. On the contrary, it might be easier to say what places aren't haunted, since the island teems with ghostly denizens. The sandy road of Howard Street is known to harbor a woman in a frayed dress. She walks among the trees and old family graves, always looking, but always hiding from the living. Farther away, in the large Howard family cemetery, next to the British cemetery holding the remains of sailors from the torpedoed *HMS Bedfordshire*, there is a resident ghost named Mad Mag Howard, who haunts the graveyard and the road nearby. Mad Mag was kidnapped by John Simon Howard and brought to Ocracoke, where she enjoyed the life of a wild tempest of a woman who was the eccentric of the island. She seems to have also stuck around in death to torment others. Later at night, a deep sea diver shuffles through the dusty night, his suit dragging him down, never reaching his boat and the water beneath.

Ocracoke offers a nice daytime trip, or a good peaceful overnight visit. As far as the ghosts go, people that stay through the night will have a chance to stroll through the empty roads in the dark of the evening and see if the ghosts really come out.

Southern Coast

Hammock House

Beaufort   34.71344° -76.65529°

A sailor may be truly at peace at the sea, but every seafarer would look forward to putting feet onto dry land. Beaufort grew up from a little village called Fish Town that was an early settlement for sheltering sailing ships and their crews. In the early 1700s, sailors would spend their dry land time in the village, with houses similar to the West Indies Bahama homes going up on whatever flat land was close by.

Hammock House was born in that way. The oldest house in Beaufort was built on a swale of high land, or hammock, right on the shore of the old Topsail Inlet, as both a spot with a good view, and as an attraction of sorts. Ships would spot the two story white house and use it as an aiming point while entering the harbor, and the building may even have been used as an inn, attracting the itinerant sailors to spend the night. The place may even have attracted the worst kind of seagoing riffraff in the infamous pirate, Blackbeard. The nefarious brigand allegedly hanged one of his many common law wives, an 18 year old French girl, in the back yard. Later uses included not only a home for seafarers throughout the years, but also as a billet for Union officers during the occupation of Beaufort throughout the Civil War. And it seems that many of the residents have left an ethereal mark on the place.

Blackbeard's wife had an unhappy end at a rope and a tree, and it is said that her screams can still be heard from the back of the house late at night. Other tales speak of a slave who took the ultimate revenge upon a cruel master, Richard Russell, a sea captain, who tried to beat the poor slave. The prisoner turned the tide and threw Russell down the stairs, snapping the man's neck and killing him.

The stairs hold other bloodthirsty tales. A sea captain returned from a long voyage, delayed by storms and struggle, only to find his fiancée in high spirits having a party. Angered that he was not missed, he rushed to the house. The captain saw a man kissing his fiancée on the cheek, and, already angered, he quickly drew his sword to deal death with the man. While guests and his fiancée yelled and tried to intervene, the two clashed, and crew held the others back. The poor man at the business end of the captain's anger slipped at the top of the stairs and tumbled down. The captain came upon him with his sword and drove it through the heart of his victim. Without a word or look, he and his crew left the house, never to return. Sadly, the man turned out to be his fiancée's brother, and they shared only a familial kiss of affection. Blood from the deed still stains the bottom steps.

Even the relative protection of occupation and a uniform had no effect. Three Union soldiers were murdered outside the house when they went there to find accommodations during the long occupation of Beaufort. After going there, no one had ever seen them again. They had long been missing and presumed dead until 1915 when their remains were finally found in the back yard.

Hammock House exudes a strangeness to visitors and residents alike. In addition to the screams of Blackbeard's victim, the sound of a girl crying has been heard. The stains at the bottom of the stairs will not clean off. Orbs and mists have been seen in the darkness. The house is popular to photograph at night in hopes of catching some evidence of a haunting. With that in mind, this house is privately owned. It is on several historic and haunted tours, but visitors do not get to go in or explore the grounds. Most of the time it will just be groups of people out walking at night instead of ghosts floating around the place. It can be photographed from the road.

Old Burying Ground

Beaufort   34.7181° -76.66395°

Beaufort is an old fishing village that grew up in the safe shelter of the inland waterways just off of the southern barrier islands of the Outer Banks. Sailors and fishermen came from the tropics to settle there, building West Indies style houses in the little town. A twelve block plan was laid out in 1712, making Beaufort the third oldest town in North Carolina.

Because of this, Beaufort has some of the oldest and strangest cemeteries in the state as well. A life on the sea rarely promised a life long lived, and even dry land, if the town could be called that, was no guarantee of safety when storms rolled in. Time and tide have always been unstoppable, and the Old Burying Ground is living and dying proof of that.

The cemetery rests between the First Baptist Church and the Anne Street United Methodist Church, under a swath of tangled old trees that have been twisted by the coastal winds. The shaded spot protects graves from as far back as 1731, and there may be remains unmarked from before that time from wars with native tribes. The earliest graves were covered with shells and bricks, partly because stone markers would have been too expensive to bring in, but also in order to protect the bodies from marauding wild animals as well as to keep them in the ground in case of a rising tide. Those are only the beginning of a series of unique graves that cover the many different souls in this lot.

Famous residents include Otway Burns, a naval privateer of the War of 1812, whose tomb is topped by one of his cannon from his ship, the *Snap Dragon*. Vienna Dill died as a child of only two years old, a victim of yellow fever. The girl was placed in a glass topped coffin and buried in the cemetery. Her beautiful visage was preserved in the coffin until vandals dug her up to see the body through the glass. Upon seeing her perfectly preserved state, they opened the casket only to have the girl's remains turn to dust at the first whiff of air. A British officer died while onboard a ship in the harbor. In order to honor his service to his country, he was buried standing up facing his home in England, forever at attention even on foreign ground. Equally tragic were the deaths of the crew of the *Chrissie Wright*, who froze to death after their craft shipwrecked. They are buried in a common grave, finally at peace on a warm beach.

The most tragic of deaths to happen to a person interred at the Old Burying Ground is a morbid and sad story known as the Little Girl in the Rum Barrel. The legend tells of a sailing captain bringing his wife and infant daughter to the new World to settle in Beaufort. While the child remembers nothing of her life in England, her mother continues to wax nostalgic for her former home. As the years pass, the girl wishes to see with her own eyes the wonders of the home she never knew, the place for which her mother's heart still beats. Her father, knowing the rigors of life at sea, and knowing a seafaring trip of months is no place for a child, refuses to take her, only to have the girl plead even more. He finally relents, and takes the girl back to

England. She finds the country and big city of London fascinating, and is in awe of the modern functions of the land, compared to simple quiet Beaufort. But she and her father must return. He had promised her mother that no matter what, he would return her back to her home. He would be sure to keep the promise, even in the direst of times.

The girl would get sick within a week of being on the ship. With no medical help available, she would die at the beginning of the journey back to the New World. Not wanting to break his promise, the captain would have the girl's remains placed into a barrel of rum to preserve it. Normally a death would mean a quick burial at sea, but the captain had given his word to his wife, her mother. It would take months for the ship to arrive, and the captain had to break the sorrowful news to his wife that their daughter had returned.

Not wanting her to see the state of their daughter, the family kept the rum barrel sealed, and buried the girl in the graveyard, with a simple wooden marker.

The story was so touching, sad and elegant, that the Little Girl in a Rum Barrel became famous over time. People would come to her grave to place flowers, then toys and trinkets, to honor the child who saw her past on the last trip, but never would have a future.

And now, people say she walks the Old Burying Ground. In the evening, as the shade pulls its dark blanket over the final resting place of the many souls in the Old Burying Ground, the girl comes out, a cloudy childlike form that walks about the tree stumps and grave markers. Her toys have been found moved, even on still nights, after the graveyard is locked. Her ghost has finally settled on a home for her, and in death she seems to have found the life that was taken as a child.

The Old Burying Ground is in the heart of Beaufort, and is part of many tours, or can be visited during the day when the gates are opened. It is locked up in the evening. Also, be warned that ghosts aren't the only thing that may get you there. During the summer, the area is full of mosquitoes. It also can get oppressively hot and humid.

Webb Library

Morehead City   34.72066° -76.71397°

T he Earl J. Webb, Jr. Memorial Library and Civic Center is a popular place for the locals of Morehead City to spend a quiet day reading and researching, though they might flinch at the name. They just call it The Webb. Built in 1929 as a commercial building for doctor's offices downstairs and a garment factory above, it became a small library for the local Woman's Club when the garment manufacturers left. From there it became a memorial to the son of its founders, Mr. and Mrs. Earl Webb. During the day it is a happy, well organized local library.

At night...

The Webb is notorious for its hauntings. Once the place closes up and the lights go out, the ghosts come out. Yes, there is more than one. A spectral fisherman has been seen to walk the library, and paranormal investigations have discovered at least one man and one woman may haunt the building. Among the usual events of a haunt, doors slamming, lights turning on by themselves after hours, ghostly footsteps and the like, there are other, more curious, and scary events.

Books have been removed from shelves, sometimes mangled or destroyed, or stacked in a different place. Paranormal groups have detected talking during electronic voice phenomena recordings. The library has areas of high electromagnetic fields, especially in the basement. The basement is not original to the library, as the building was constructed upon the foundation of a much older house, with the original basement below. The library also has mysterious cold spots, areas where oddly frigid air will remain even without a source, such as a window or vent.

And most peculiar is the tale of something dreadful making a foul disgusting smell in the library. No one could find the source of the smell, though it permeated the building so badly that the library was closed. It later went away as mysteriously as it came.

The strange part is that no one can determine why the Webb is haunted, only that it definitely is. There may be hints of something even more unimaginable than just a couple of ghosts there. Something more unspeakable, lurking in the depths.

The library is open and accepting to people who want to know more about the haunted building, and have allowed various investigations. There is even a tour available for novice ghost hunters. Just beware the basement. It seems even the ghosts don't want anyone down there.

Fort Macon

Atlantic Beach 34.69788° -76.67849°

The coast of North Carolina is now just a destination for worshipers of sun and sand, the families looking to escape the trap of their daily lives the other 51 weeks of the year. But as far back as 1747 the coast of Atlantic Beach was a prime spot for a naval attack. Spanish, English, and even pirate invaders have unwillingly graced the area over several decades. It became obvious that the area was in high need of fortification.

Fort Macon was the third fort built in the area to defend the port and inlet to Beaufort, in response to the second fort, Fort Hampton, being shown to be weak to improving assault techniques, as well as because the fort was being swallowed up by the ever encroaching inlet.

The current fort was occupied by Union forces at the beginning of the Civil War, only to be taken over by a North Carolina militia. Then, during General Burnside's march down the coast, he seized Beaufort without a shot. Fort Macon was not so easily taken, and withstood both a naval attack and an advance on land, before suffering the fire of over 500 rifled shells. The damage was so severe that the fort finally was surrendered, again changing hands of power.

Now only the ghosts of history walk the parapets of the fort. Even with continual threats a thing of the past, the soldiers that served there are still prepared to face off against an attack that will no longer come. A ghost has been seen walking the ramparts, along with shadows and footsteps inside the fort. Doors close unexpectedly, including the time when soldiers manning the fort during World War II saw the front gates close and lock on their own.

But the most haunting, and tragic, story, involves the ghost of the parapet. A singular spectral figure has been seen to walk the fortifications in the evening. Legend tells that it is the ghost of Ben Combs, a young Wayne County farmer, who joined other North Carolinians to defend his state from invasion. He marched with others to serve as pickets and sentinels at the fort. He probably was unaware of the horrors of war right up until the time the first shells fell on the fort. And he wouldn't be aware of anything for much longer. During the attack on the fort, a shell fell next him and exploded. It mortally wounded the inexperienced soldier, though it took him days to die from his injuries.

Over a hundred years later, his identity was discovered by a psychic visiting the fort. Now people come to look for him. One of the early victims of war still is trying to serve even though he knew little about being a soldier. Combs is usually spotted in the twilight, walking the grounds, with a rifle over his shoulder. No one has been able to photograph him. Maybe he just wants to do the job he was supposed to do over a century ago.

Visiting Fort Macon is easy, if you visit during the day. The park is open 9-5:30 daily, and it includes a beach area during the warmer months. Visiting in the evening is more difficult, if ghost hunters expect to see a ghost. Paranormal investigators have arranged to camp out in the fort overnight in hopes of spotting a spectral soldier.

Cotton Exchange

Wilmington   34.2394° -77.94985°

Wilmington's Cotton Exchange is a collection of historical buildings saved from destruction in the 1970s when the port town was going through an economic downturn after the numerous businesses, including the Atlantic Coastline Railroad, closed up or left the city. Many buildings were being torn down for redevelopment, as it was cheaper than refurbishing the older, already standing ones. However, the buildings of the Cotton Exchange were  saved when a partnership bought the buildings and renovated them with a classic coastal feel.

The buildings consisted of several businesses from the late 1800s until the 1950s. The Cotton Exchange was actually the James Sprunt Cotton Exchange, the largest exporter of cotton on the east coast. In addition to other businesses there was a boarding house, a public house, and a brothel.

The new owners wanted to create a historic old building, with the experience of modern shopping. Little would they know just how far back that historic experience would go. The Cotton Exchange has been a popular place with ghosts for a long time.

Top Toad, a t-shirt and clothing store, has an active spirit who unfolds shirts and knocks over the store's displays. The Scoop has a mischievous girl who likes to play with all the ice cream equipment and run her invisible hands along the wind chimes. She only appears as a reflection, in the glass of the ice cream case or in a clock face on the wall.

The German Café and Paddy's Hollow may share a ghostly couple of sorts. The German Café has had a woman grace the building, dressed in Victorian clothing as she walks the stores. She has redecorated one of the stores in the building, and has been known to slam windows closed even when no one can be seen.

Her male counterpart haunts Paddy's Hollow, the local pub. Tall and dressed all in black, he wanders through, literally, the bar, disappearing into walls without a trace. Some think he may be tied into an old graveyard nearby, a tender of the long gone bone orchard, or a pallbearer waiting for his next job.

Visiting the Cotton exchange is easy, since it is a set of shops open for people to come in and buy something. Exploring and looking around is a fun exercise. The buildings have a wonderful modern/old mix of feelings, and the little hidden passageways keep visitors looking over their shoulders, waiting for a ghost from Wilmington's past to walk by, brush a shoulder, tug lightly on a cuff of a shirt. One place may be as good as another to see a ghost, but considering people can either get ice cream or one of their favorite adult beverages at a couple of the places ghosts are seen, well, make your choices accordingly.

St. James Episcopal Church

Wilmington 34.23514° -77.94473°

The cold winds of winter would not chill the anger of Samuel Jocelyn. Furious with his wife, he left in the middle of the night on his horse to ride away through the cold wet swamps of Honey Island. A rash decision, but bitterness would cloud good judgment. It would also cloud his vision, as Samuel would strike a heavy tree branch in the blackness, knocking him from his horse, rendering him unconscious in the muddy ground. He would not be noticed missing until the next day. When he was found, his body was discovered face down, frozen in the icy water of the swamp.

In the year 1810, there was little in the way of coronary medicine. There was no doubt that Samuel Jocelyn had been struck hard in the head, that he had fallen from his horse, and that he had lain in freezing water for a day motionless. There was also no doubt that he was surely dead, and the dead of the time did not interact well with the living since there were no preserving properties used on dead bodies. The best solution was to get the body into the ground as quickly as possible. Which is why a grave was quickly dug at St. James Episcopal Church for

Samuel Jocelyn's remains. His body was laid to rest, mourners, including his friends, did the best they could to grieve, and they moved on as the coffin was covered with dirt.

This would seem like the end of Samuel Jocelyn's short and unfortunate life. It would be appropriate at this time for his friends to lament on his passing, to pass their minds back to moments with him, but something more happened. Two of his closest friends both had dreams where Samuel appeared, pleading with them that he had been buried alive. He begged for them to come save him. After the second night of this happening, the two men met, both astonished to find they had the same dream, and the same intent. They were both headed to the graveyard to put to rest the dream that haunted their nights.

They dug up the coffin and opened it. Instead of finding a body at peace, they found a horrendous sight. Samuel's face was frozen in horror, eyes wide and frantic. His body sat in a pool of his own blood. His fingers had been worn down to the bone, the sanguine fluid dripping down his arms to fill the coffin. He had awoke in his own coffin, terrified at the discovery. In the blackness he had scratched at the lid in the vain hope of opening the coffin and digging through six feet of cold hard earth to escape his grave. Only after exhausting his energy and all the air he had did Samuel Jocelyn finally succumb to death.

Afterward, and for centuries now, near an unmarked headstone, a shadow appears in the quiet dusk. It leans over the stone, as if to mourn the life that was trapped below. At midnight, Samuel has made a different kind of appearance. The witching hour brings the screams of terror as Samuel wakes up to find himself trapped, and his cries can be heard across the graveyard.

Sadly, this was not an entirely exceptional event. In the time before decent medical care, if someone looked dead, they were assumed that they probably were dead. A very weak pulse or shallow breath could easily be hidden behind a bash in the head and a nearly frozen body. Since the dead did not mix well with the living, due to the quick decomposition of the body, they were often placed into the ground as soon as possible.

The fear of being buried alive was a known threat. Many people went to great lengths to make sure that didn't happen to them. Strings tied to fingers that would first stir would lead up through the ground to bells where diligent watchers would wait and listen. The concerned would literally work the graveyard shift, sitting a quiet night, in both hope and fear, of hearing the sound of a bell ringing, and of not hearing the screams from deeper below.

The original Episcopal Church was replaced in 1839. The graves remain from the first church, though time has worn away the names of many of the first residents planted there. The graveyard can be seen through the fence behind the church on 4th Street. Legends tell of other ghosts that walk the graveyard. It may be one of the most haunted cemeteries in the state.

Bellamy Mansion

Wilmington 34.23607° -77.94278°

Looking at his numerous successful businesses, a surplus of money, and a large and growing family, Dr. John Bellamy looked around at his home on Dock Street in Wilmington, the same home of former governor Benjamin Smith, and decided he needed a larger, grander space to serve the needs of his family, with all the servants and slaves that attended them. In 1859 he would begin to design and build the Bellamy Mansion, a 22 room home that would ultimately hold 9 of his 10 children, his wife, servants, and Bellamy himself.

The house would be finished in 1861, an ominous date for Wilmingtonians and southerners, though Bellamy wouldn't know it at the time. The Civil War would always be at the shore near Wilmington, but Yellow Fever would first pass through the city, sending the Bellamy family inland to their plantation for the relative safety from the disease. By the time Fort Fisher would fall and the Union Army would occupy the port city, the newly built Bellamy House would be used as headquarters for the Union. Even after the war, it would prove difficult to get the home back into the Bellamy's hands. It wouldn't be until September of 1865 that the family would regain ownership and begin to move back in.

The house would stay occupied by a child of Dr. Bellamy until 1946. Even during the decay and restoration efforts afterward, the house stayed in the Bellamy family hands. Only after it was turned over to Preservation North Carolina and became a museum and community event center was the Bellamy family free of the property.

However, since the property was so beautiful and so loved by the Bellamys that they seem to have stuck around.

Ghosts abound in the house. Most of them are family members, including Dr. and Mrs. Bellamy. Most of these are discovered through EVP studies at the mansion. Dr. Bellamy seems to respond tersely, not happy to have others in his home. While his wife has made herself known to be more pleasant. This could come from the time of the Union occupation of their home. Dr. Bellamy was not happy about the generals using his home when had so little use of it himself at the time. His wife Eliza was genteel and ladylike, even being noted for her politeness to Mrs. Harriet Hawley, wife of Gen. Joseph Hawley, who occupied the house. Children and servants also make their presence known. The slave house, which would later hold servants, also has some presence of a ghost in it.

The only visible presence that may be seen is a possible ghost on the top floor. Only a few people have even mentioned seeing it, an ethereal woman in a long dress that disappears as soon as she is seen.

The house will be difficult to investigate as it is a public museum during the day, with guided and self guided tours going on until 5 pm. It may be hard to separate the living and the dead when doing recordings or photos. Also, Bellamy Mansion doesn't encourage the promotion of the ghostly legends. Most public buildings don't. They have allowed private groups to come in and do investigations, but may not let just anyone in off the street to spend the night there.

Thalian Hall

Wilmington

34.23715° -77.94564°

During the 1850s, when the age of sailing brought goods from all over the world to its ports, Wilmington was the largest city in the state, and a mecca for theater and high culture. Built between 1855 and 1858, Thalian Hall would hold 1,000 people. It was large enough to hold one out of every ten people in the city. Once finished, it attracted major touring shows, and was in constant use until the Civil War. It has been a near constant showpiece for the city ever since.

The grandiose theater has been popular with both actors and patrons for over 150 years. Most of the time they come and go with the shows that are on stage. Three guests have stayed a little longer.

Sporting top hats and a bonnet, respectively, two men and one woman in ritzy attire have been seen sitting in the center of the balcony while actors rehearse onstage. Hidden in the shadows and behind the bright lights, they have been spied by thespians as they trod the boards of Thalian Hall. No one knows who the three are. Even suspicions or theories have been kept to a minimum. Thalian

Hall itself, by way of its management, lightheartedly denies the existence of the ghosts, blaming any otherworld events on Thalia herself, the muse of comedy. They do agree that there are tales told about the place, cold spots, whispers in the darkness, and the movement of items from the stage without anyone noticing.

Seeing the ghosts would prove to be difficult. They are usually seen from stage, by the actors, so the best chance is to be in a performance. Thalian Hall does book private group tours, and may be open to having some ghost hunters come in. The best way is to go see a play. The ghosts probably won't appear, but at least the show will be good.

USS North Carolina

Wilmington   34.23607° -77.95364°

With the expansion of dangerous powers on both oceans in the 1930s, the United States needed a new class of battleship that could handle even the long distance crossing of the acutely misnamed Pacific and still be ready to deliver destruction on a moment's notice. The *USS North Carolina* was the first of many battleships to come, and when she was finally fitted out for war, the *North Carolina* was the biggest bully on the block.

Since she was the first of her kind, the *North Carolina* saw action in the Pacific from Guadalcanal to Okinawa and beyond to the home islands of Japan. During the battle of the Eastern Solomons, while guarding the aircraft carrier *USS Enterprise*, the battleship put up so many rounds into the air in a short 8 minute shootout with Japanese aircraft, shooting down about 14 airplanes, the antiaircraft fire from the *North Carolina* was so thick that the *Enterprise* had to radio the battleship, "Are you afire?" Due to the ability for the *North Carolina* to put forth such a performance, it earned the nickname The Showboat during its career in the Pacific Theater. The *USS North Carolina* earned 15 battle stars for its service.

The crew was, generally, fortunate to serve aboard the ship. Only ten sailors lost their lives in battle, with five of them coming during a torpedo strike at Guadalcanal, the only time the ship received major damage.

A couple of the sailors have left their spirits with the ship in some way. The *North Carolina* has been rather dependable in spectral performance over the years. One or two ghosts seem to inhabit the ship, with various ways of displaying their presence. More often spotted is a blond sailor, sometimes seen as white haired, who appears and disappears both day and night. He has been seen by visitors on tours of the ship, his face appearing in portholes or in glass, as well as his full body, opaque, floating in the hallways. He also appears at night to ghost hunters and the night watchers that serve as security onboard. Danny Bradshaw has worked as the night watchman for decades and has spotted the blond sailor more than once. He described the figure more as white, with hair aflame, rather than a blond, and he doesn't seem to relish the ghost's appearances. This ghost also likes to play with the electronics onboard, turning TVs and monitors on, as well as moving items, knocking things off tables, and just finding different ways to make him known.

There may be another presence on the ship. In addition to the usual noises that could either be attributed to an old ship, even sitting still, there have been doors opening, footfalls, items falling or becoming detached. Some ghost hunters find their equipment acting up or being turned off. Shadows appear where there are no people walking to cut through the soft lights used late at night onboard. Some investigators, and Bradshaw, report another spirit that, while not entirely malevolent, seems to be decidedly unhappy. This ghost does not manifest itself as much, nor as well.

The *USS North Carolina* is currently a museum ship, and can be visited every day of the year. Tickets are needed, and the ship closes up, for the living, at 5pm. It's also set up a lot like it was when it was at war, which means it doesn't have air conditioning. Visitors will need to dress appropriately, with good shoes for going up and down those ladders, and lots of water in the summer. Take the cameras in case a ghost pops out, but keep them on a strap.

Maco Light

Maco 34.27613° -78.12381°

Joe Baldwin rose from his chair at the rear of his train heading into Wilmington. The sun had already set over the line to the west, and twilight had crept its way through the sky, turning the heavens a deep violet, with the night's lanterns turning on in the inky darkness. It was his job to announce the next stop in the Wilmington and Manchester Railroad, which was the station at Maco, a small town near Leland. An experienced conductor of the road, Baldwin noticed something was wrong immediately. His car had become uncoupled from the rest of the train. It slowed on the tracks as the other cars continued on down the rails. He knew that the next train to pass would be a speeding express, not stopping at the spurs of the little towns his train would normally stop. Knowing the imminent danger, as the caboose coasted down the tracks, he grabbed his lantern and raced to the back of the car, where he began swinging his light in earnest but fruitless hope of warning the approaching express train.

Sadly, his steadfast devotion did nothing to stop the other train. It plowed into his tiny car at full speed. Joe was impacted by the engine, sending his lantern flying into the swamp. He was killed immediately, with his head separated from his body. The other train derailed but no one was lost in the accident besides poor Joe.

After the accident, Joe's body was found in the wreckage, but his head was never discovered. It was thought to have disappeared into the murky swamp along the rail line. Joe's mortal remains were buried in Wilmington, the honored dead who did his duty and gave his life.

Not long after, a couple who were walking hand in hand during the evening passed by the place where the train accident happened. In the darkness they saw it; a bobbing light appeared over the empty tracks, swaying side to side. But no hand held the light, no arm swung a lantern, just a light, floating in the ether.

Over time, others saw the light. It was soon theorized that the light was from poor Joe Baldwin. Joe walked the tracks as a ghost, still looking for his head.

This happened in 1867, and people had been seeing Joe Baldwin's light for the next 100 years. President Grover Cleveland saw the light in 1889 on a stop during a visit to Wilmington. By the 1930s newspapers were reporting on the light regularly. *Life* magazine did an article on it in 1957. During the boom of car travel in the state in the 1950s and 60s, tourists to the Cape Fear coast would often make the trip up to Maco, stop by the side of the road, and wait to see the light. More often than not, they weren't disappointed. A strange flare of light would appear in the darkness above the rails, streaking through the air. It would float and bob across the tracks, slowly approaching the watchers, who may or may not choose to stay to see how close it will get. The Army even got involved when a colonel gathered some of his men to track down and surround the light. They encircled it, only to have the glowing orb disappear from their midst and have it reappear outside of the circle and continue bobbing its way down the tracks.

So prevalent was the light's appearance that people would plan their trips to visit the light. Some even went so far to go out with nets in the vain hope of catching it. The light appeared often, and besides the legend of Joe Baldwin, more mundane ideas of the light were put forth. Some thought it was just swamp gas igniting in the marsh next to the railroad. Others proclaimed it was the reflection of passing car and truck headlights, somehow shimmering off the swamp and its strange vapors. Most people didn't buy the explanations, with the light's ability to move down the tracks, and its documented legend before cars travelled the road.

In 1977, the rail lines were abandoned and pulled up. With the destruction of the railroad line, Joe Baldwin also disappeared. It was thought that Joe's ghost finally knew the road would be safe now that no trains travelled the tracks. The Legend of Joe Baldwin and Maco Light became just that, a legend. The light was gone.

Or, maybe not. North Carolina paranormal investigators N.C. H.A.G.S. were able to get permission and local guidance to do an investigation of the area. They found the remains of the old depot, and did a night investigation. No lights appeared, but they did detect a strange figure in the darkness, which looked a lot like a human. There could be a little bit of Joe Baldwin hidden somewhere deep in those forbidding woods.

Don't go looking for the light. It no longer appears. Locals do not like people snooping, and will call the police on trespassers. Too many times have unscrupulous trespassers littered and damaged the area. It also became a popular spot as a lover's lane for a time. Even in the day, residents will not be welcoming of people prowling around the land. And neither will their dogs.

Fort Fisher

Kure Beach 33.97183° -77.91753°

The inlet to the Cape Fear, with the port city of Wilmington beyond, was so precious and beneficial to the southern states that the Confederacy built a deadly jewel of a defensive fortification at its entrance. Fort Fisher was a marvel for the time. It was designed by Col. William Lamb out of sand and earth, in order to withstand the most massive of impacts from a sea barrage. The north land side was peppered with torpedoes, early electric mines, to ward off any attack. So feared was the fort that no attempt at taking the fort was done until the end of the Civil War, when more and more defenders had been taken from the fort to fight in other battles. It would take a massive attack from the ocean and land to finally have the fort, the Gibraltar of the South, fall the advancing Union onslaught.

Today the fort is a state park, and a popular place for fishing or going to the beach. The guns are long gone. Most of the rolling earthen mounds are long gone, with only a percentage preserved for people to get a feel of what the fort may have been like. The twisted trees grow up into a delicate maritime forest, the timber being pushed and turned by the salty wind that blows off the Atlantic. Mornings bring the clear yellow sunrise that flows into beautiful blue days. Waves lap the shore, where the footprints of invasion have long been washed away.

But when the sun sets, the shadows grow long in the oaks and pines that grew up where soldiers once fell. The park closes, the people pack up and go home, it gets dark, and then the ghosts come out.

A singular figure appears on the fourth mound, looking north. The gray clad man stares out into the darkness, on guard for the attack he already knows is coming, because it already happened. The ghost of Gen. William Whiting saw the battle long ago, and it cost him his freedom and his life. Whiting was in charge of the fort until drinking problems and personal issues placed General Braxton Bragg over him at Fort Fisher. When the attack came, Whiting saw his fort fall, and he was captured. He died while imprisoned. Legend says that with his dying breath, he cursed Bragg for letting the fort fall to the Union.

So, even today, General Whiting still stands at the parapet, looking north, awaiting the attack that has already come and gone. It is his ghost's hope that this time he can somehow prevail. His ghost has been seen numerous times, always standing or walking the top of the mound.

Deeper into the woods, the new trees that grew up where the land mines once sat buried, ghostly figures have been seen wandering through the trees. Soldiers have crept from spot to spot, crouching to avoid the bullets and shrapnel of war. A spectral horse has even been heard, clopping and snorting softly. Gunshots and the sound of war have been heard in the darkness. Cold spots appear, as do feelings of dread and fear. In the blackness, ghost hunters have felt watchful eyes of spirits that are not visible.

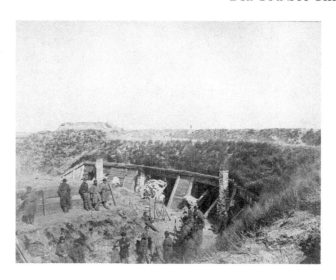

The fort is open during the day until 5pm, with no fees. There is also a beach and parking area nearby. The park no longer allows access at night for ghost hunting, and the popular spot may be tainted by people out at night faking ghostly visits. As a historic visit, it is well worth the trip to Pleasure Island, and a great part of a summer vacation.

Brunswick Inn

Southport   33.91849° -78.01533°

There are ghostly legends, and then there are ghosts. Legends are mostly tales of an event, with little to connect it to present day, even if there is some remainder of the occurrence, or the dregs of the tale still exist in some way. A ghost is just that, a spirit, an apparition. A ghost is the manifestation of what is left after a person leaves this world behind.

That's more of what Tony, the ghost of the Brunswick Inn B&B, is like.

Tony is Antonio Casaletta, a young Italian who immigrated to the U.S. and moved to Southport in hopes of getting a job as a musician. He found happy employment at the inn, playing a harp with other musicians in a band there, to the guests' pleasure. Tony and his bandmates would do things together on their off time, enjoying the mild weather and the wonderful explorations that could be had along the coast. One day he and the rest of his band went out sailing. In the years before adequate weather prediction, a storm could blow up without warning, and this is just what happened to Antonio's boat. As a result Antonio drowned in the waters off Southport. His body was recovered and interred in the Old Smythville Burying Ground.

Antonio, or Tony, may have parted with his mortal remains, but his spirit seems too happy to leave the inn. Tony died at only 19, and wanted to stick around to enjoy the job he got, doing what he loved. Legend even tells that in Tony's honor, the band played that night, but left his seat empty out of respect. When the band began to perform, the harp began to play, all by itself.

Tony has continued to haunt, in a kindly way, the halls and rooms of the Brunswick Inn since his passing. Tony will turn on lights, and close windows when the rains roll in off the waters that feed into the Atlantic. He even got the quilts out for the owners' children when the nights first got cold.

Guests have had their own experiences with Tony. Being a young man, he likes to play tricks and pranks, like sneaking open suitcases and throwing out all the socks and undergarments. Tony also likes to play with ladies' jewelry.

The good thing is that if someone wants to experience Tony's playful haunting, it is pretty easy to do so. Simply book a room at the Inn. The Brunswick Inn is open year round to adults. The rooms are nice, quaint, old style, and fit for a couple, but it isn't well set up for kids, and does not offer family rooms. What visitors will get is a nice view of the waters, a good base for visiting Southport or Oak Island and beyond, and quite possibly a visit from a prankster harpist.

Captain Charlie's

Bald Head Island   33.84662° -77.96589°

Bald Head Island could have gone the way of rapid growth, with high rise hotels, big beach houses, and a four lane bridge spanning the waters, but luckily, it didn't. Instead most of the island was put into preserve, with a modest and sedate development on the island, where people take their time, riding golf carts or walking, or just not doing anything. Bald Head Island is beachfront bliss at its pinnacle.

The island has always been a natural barrier island, but the barrier part has made it as famous as the natural look the island has. Long before tourists and vacationers came, the island was popular with pirates, when both Blackbeard and Stede Bonnet found the place to be useful as a hideout. And the offshore Frying Pan Shoals were notorious to reach up and grab a ship by its hull and leave it stranded on the soft sand floor. Old Baldy, the small lighthouse on the west side of the island, was only meant to mark the channel entrance. In the early 1900s, a tall skeletal tower with a light was built out on the point to warn off ships. And with it came a set of cottages as lighthouse keepers' quarters. And it is in these houses that the island's ghosts still reside.

Now rental cottages, they are known as Captain Charlie's Cottages, are available for vacations. Renters may find someone already there. Two ghosts, a man and a woman, have each been seen in the cottages. A red haired woman named Mrs. Cloden resides in one, or all, houses at some time. She was the victim of a shipwreck, and was stranded in one of the houses, where she slowly died of starvation. She makes herself felt more as a presence, or a feeling, than in actual appearance as a ghost. Animals may be more sensitive to her than humans.

Another ghost that has made some form a visible appearance is the man in the pin striped suit. The fact that people can see him wearing a pin striped suit means that he must have been seen. He is spotted, silent, staring out of the window looking over the water of Frying Pan Shoals. Little is known of the man; he merely appears, a well dressed apparition, with a mask of ennui on his ghostly face.

Finding the ghosts, depending on luck in the first place to actually see one, is going to be time consuming and costly. Getting to the island is by passenger ferry or private boat, and the preferred mode of travel is golf cart or bike, along with hoofing it. Captain Charlie's cabins are steeply priced for rustic cottages, but the location on the end of the beach demands the premium price. Summer fills up quickly, but Bald Head Island is a great spot to spend a week, ghost or no ghost.

Ghosts' Second Homes

A Spooky Side Trip

In addition to the ghosts that haunt the homes of Southport, or the beaches of Bald Head Island, there are other legends of spooky appearances in the Brunswick County area that show up from time to time. The difficult issue is, they seem to have another, more permanent, home somewhere else. They could be on vacation. They could be a different ghost.

Theodosia Burr Allston is known to walk her plantation in South Carolina, and her strange disappearance has lead to tales of her ghost in many other places, all the way up into Virginia. Her ghost has allegedly appeared on Bald Head Island, with the tale that her ship was actually seized at Bald Head, then set adrift only to wash ashore in Nags Head. Her ghost appeared so regularly that a B&B took her name at the place where she appears.

Toward the west, at Oak Island, the Gray Man has walked. The Gray Man has also walked along the beaches of Hatteras and most famously Pawleys Island. He warns of a pending storm to whoever sees him, protecting the homes of his viewers.

The area is ripe with spooks. Just make sure to enjoy the mundane vistas of sandy beaches, warm water, and beautiful sunsets, too.

The Winds Resort

Ocean Isle   33.89405° -78.41095°

L ittle is known about this ghost legend. The tale is often repeated verbatim. Sam was a guest at the Winds Resort, and he had a heart attack and died in one of the rooms. Now his ghost haunts the room. He will open and close the blinds in the windows. Guests and employees report cold spots in the cabin where he died.

The problem with the story is that it is almost always told the same way. There is no last name, no date, nothing more than a general heart attack cause of death. The story seems to have attached itself from one report and has been repeated over and over, with no new additions as the legend has been made clearer.

Perhaps a visit to the cabin will reveal something. Perhaps extra sunscreen and a long day at the beach would be just as productive.

Coastal Plain

Nell Cropsey House

Elizabeth City 36.29397° -76.20808°

As a ghost story, the haunting of the Cropsey house is pretty standard fare. As a murder mystery, it is certainly a unique and sensational tale indeed.

The Cropsey family arrived in Elizabeth City in 1898, father William and mother Mary Louise, with their three children in tow, from Brooklyn, NY. Locals were abuzz with the newly arrived residents from up north, especially young Ella Maud Cropsey, who went by the name Nell. At 16 years old, she was a stunningly beautiful young girl. Locals about the town all competed to court Nell, but she chose, somewhat oddly to many, Jim Wilcox, who was the son of the local sheriff, and five years senior to the teenage girl. Wilcox was seen as not only a strange choice, but just strange. Why she chose him, there was little understanding, but the two seemed to hit it off.

Nell and Wilcox dated for three years, and the girl grew into a young woman. Wilcox may have aged, but he didn't seem to grow as much. Nell was now 19 and wanted Jim Wilcox to step up and plan for their next part of life together by getting engaged. On November 20, 1901, Nell was heard in a heated argument with her beau. No one could make out what was being said, but everyone knew. It was Nell finally having it out with Wilcox. And Wilcox was giving it back. Nell had grown tired of waiting for him, and had been actively flirting with other men around town in order to get Wilcox jealous. He argued back to her about her actions. Though the two supposedly patched things up, when she later walked out onto the porch with him that night, it would be the last time Nell Cropsey was seen alive.

Later that night, the family would be awakened by the frantic calls of a neighbor. Someone was in the back of their house, trying to steal a pig from the back yard. Everyone in the house came out to see the commotion. Everyone except Nell. Nell was missing.

The next day the town came out looking for the beautiful Nell. The one person who didn't want to look was Jim Wilcox. Of course, with the two of them fighting the night before and he being the last person to see her alive meant that he was a prime suspect, and he was arrested almost immediately.

Nell wouldn't be found that day. Or then next. It wouldn't be until 37 days later, after Christmas, that her body would be found. Her mother, Mary, would wake up that morning to look across the nearby Pasquotank River and see something floating in the water. A boat was sent out, and Mary would see from afar as her daughter's body would be pulled aboard. Nell was finally found.

A curious occurrence happened at about the same time as the discovery of Nell's body. A note was sent, accusing a vagrant of killing Nell when he was out trying to steal the pig late that night. It even confessed as to where the body would be found. The story said that Nell had discovered the late night pig robber, and he had killed her to escape.

With the discovery of Nell's body, the town as a whole went mad. A mob descended upon the jail, demanding that Wilcox be released to them to serve up vigilante justice. Nell was well liked, and her beau Wilcox was seen as an odd person, as well as the most likely suspect. Nell's parents had to go to the jail to plead with the town to let justice take its course within the law.

It is questionable whether or not that ultimately happened.

Jim Wilcox was tried and found guilty of the murder, but later had the case overturned in the NC Supreme Court when a mistrial was declared. Retried, and with shaky circumstantial evidence, Wilcox was again found guilty, and was sentenced to 30 years in prison. He would serve until 1920, when Governor Thomas Bickett would pardon him as part of a lenient policy against the poor prison conditions in North Carolina.

Later in life, Wilcox would go to W.O. Saunders, a well respected news editor in Elizabeth City, and tell him everything he knew of Nell's death. Two weeks later, Wilcox would kill himself. Sadly, Saunders also would pass on from injuries in a car accident. Saunders said that he believed Wilcox to be innocent, but the conversation between the two would be lost to time. No one knows what was said in the interview.

With Nell's untimely and cruel death, her spirit seems to be unsatisfied with the way her life ended. In the house she lived for three years, Nell has been seen and felt. Owners tell of lights going on and off by themselves. Interior doors will slam in the closed house. Most disturbingly, the ghost of Nell Cropsey has even been seen in the house. An ethereal figure has been seen walking or floating through the home. Her visage has been spotted by neighbors or visitors in the windows of the house. Nell left her life too soon and unsatisfied with her short life. She seems to linger in the hope of fulfillment, or perhaps she is just melancholy in a life wasted by another. With no real satisfaction as to who did the crime, she may continue to walk the hallways of her home, forever.

The Cropsey house is still a private residence, but can be seen from the street. As a historical house, it is occasionally open to the public, especially for a parade of homes or Elizabeth City's ghost walk. Visitors can pass by the house on the public roads.

Earley Light

Ahoskie   36.25604° -77.02758°

Aulander   36.24102° -77.06762°

North Carolina has an abundance of strange lights that orbit the train tracks that crisscross the state. Trains were important to the state because of the poor state of roads until the 1900s. With trains moving people and products across the land, there would often be accidents, and train accidents were rarely forgiving.

Earley Light, also called Aulander Light, is a strange floating orb that appears along a straight line of track in between the towns of Ahoskie and Aulander. Earley Station is the nearby old depot location. The light appears along the track heading south from Earley Station down toward Aulander. It has been seen as a swaying, blinking light, passing slowly from side to side, disappearing at the zenith of the arc, then appearing again passing the other way. It is often described as similar to a man walking with a lantern swaying in his hand. The light is definitely not manmade, as it changes in brightness and in color, and does not look like a train nor appear when trains travel the rails. Sometimes two lights appear as well.

There are two legends attached to the light. One is the rather typical tale of a conductor losing his head in an accident, and now he walks the road, ghostly lantern in his hand, warning others of danger, or perhaps searching for his head.

There is a local tale that adds more detail to the legend. The story tells of James Pearce, the conductor of a freight train that was passing through the empty country of Hertford County late at night.

He spotted an approaching train that appeared on his line in the darkness. Somehow, the lines got mixed and two trains barreled toward each other. Pearce applied his brakes, but stopping a high speed freight train quickly is an impossible task. He did what he could to brace for the terrible impact to come. Only it never happened. As the train approached Pearce, it veered off, where no tracks sat. The train was a phantom, a ghostly line that whisked by in terrifying silence. Stunned, the conductor pushed his own train ahead, to stop at Earley Station outside of Ahoskie. Pearce stopped to write a report on the occurrence, but all the teasing by coworkers at the station made him slam the pen down and leave to continue his run.

The people that teased him would have reason to feel bad soon enough. James Pearce's train would derail up the line, killing the conductor in the crash.

Now Pearce can be seen walking the line where he saw the phantom train, waving his light side to side to watch his step. He is said to still be trying to get to Earley Station to finish the report he should have filled out. It may have saved his life.

Now people see the light appear in the darkness south of Earley Station. There are two spots to see the light. Near Ahoskie is the location of the old Earley Station, and closer to Aulander is an unmarked crossing where a local road crosses the railroad line. There are places to park nearby, but explorers will have to leave their cars in quiet empty spots to hike out along the rails. The railroad line is dangerous in the typical sense that it is still used, and trains can oddly enough sneak up on people who walk the line and don't notice a train from behind. Of equal danger is the surrounding area. Not only is the line dangerous, but it may be difficult to even step off the rails. Swamp and marsh surround the raised rail line, and the woods are home to wild animals, including black bears. Be careful to distinguish between a ghost light and a train light.

The Brown Lady of Chowan University

Murfreesboro   36.43642° -77.09916°

T he ghost of a charming debutante student walks the halls and paths of Chowan University. Clad in her fancy russet dress of lace, taffeta, and chiffon, students and faculty have heard her walk invisibly through the halls and walkways of Chowan University. Her spectral form passes in front of the McDowell Columns building, an imposing building built in 1851, one of the oldest buildings on campus.

Curiously, there is only one ghost, but two legends attached to the haunted campus.

Eolene Davidson was the beautiful teenage daughter of a local wealthy family of the farming community of Northampton County. She grew up well to do, and wanted for nothing, but she desired greatly to have an education. Her father also valued edification for his daughter, and wanted her to attend Chowan Baptist Female Institute, a school of higher learning for young women.

Before her first year in college, she went on vacation with her family to New York. The mild New York summer and different vistas did her well. She also enjoyed meeting a young man by the name of James Lorrene. James was a successful lawyer in the state, a handsome and kind man of dark eyes and tall stature. The beautiful southern brunette and the handsome attorney were a perfect match. So perfect that before the end of the summer, James had asked Eolene to marry him. And she accepted.

The only difficulty was that Eolene, and her family as well, wanted her to get an education. So a deal was struck. They would remain engaged while Eolene went to school, and would marry once she graduated.

Eolene happily attended her first year at the school, becoming well liked by the other girls at the college. She was especially known for her penchant for fancy gowns, all done up in shades of brown. She became so well known for her fancy dress that she was nicknamed "The Lady in Brown." Students would know of her coming before she appeared by the whooshing sound of her skirts as she walked down the halls. Eolene had by all accounts a very successful freshman year at Chowan.

Summer vacation came again, and this time James came down from New York to see his betrothed. The family welcomed and liked the dapper young man. The blessings of a future marriage were reinforced again, and Eolene's mother even began planning for a wedding.

The next year started the same as before. Fall came to the area, and Eolene made the most of her happy time at school, still walking the grounds and halls in her brown dresses, her skirts and petticoats whishing through the hallways. But soon she began to feel ill. By late September, she knew that she was not well. And in October of the year, she felt like there was something so seriously wrong that she summoned her fiancé to see her, fearing it would be the last time.

James Lorrene rushed from his home to be with his betrothed. There was no direct way to get to Murfreesboro, and he had to navigate a myriad maze of trains and even rides on horseback to finally get to the college. Sadly, he arrived too late. Eolene passed away before he could arrive. He had finally gotten to the college on November 1, and Eolene had died on Halloween night.

Now Eolene walks the halls, her invisible form still wearing her dress, the sound of her skirts still can be heard rustling the walls as her wide dress slides gracefully by. Students and staff have heard the noise of the Lady in Brown as she still walks the buildings of the campus. She often will either make her presence known, or even be seen, around the Columns Building, in the center of campus. Staff report finding leaves, branches, and twigs in the building in the morning after the doors have been closed for the night and the floors swept. And late in the evening, especially on Halloween night, Eolene can be seen, a misty figure still dressed in brown, walking the campus.

There is also another legend attached to the same ghost, as well. Julia is described similarly to Eolene. However, her fiancé meets a more ignominious fate. She is engaged to a successful and handsome young man, but it is the beginning of the Civil War, and he goes off to fight. Sadly for the southern belle, he fights for the Union Army. He is mortally wounded during a battle, and when Julia learns of his death, distraught, she climbs to the top of the Columns Building and flings herself to her death.

The school has embraced their ghost, honoring her and recognizing the legend with gracious acceptance. Visiting the campus is as easy as seeing any other campus, but being out at the school at night might bring more attention to a stranger than it would to a ghostly lady in brown. Enjoy the legend, but don't get a visit from campus security.

Somerset Place

Creswell 35.78745° -76.40481°

The southern beauty of an antebellum plantation that rests in peaceful splendor along the shore of a still, glassy lake is a stark disparity to the reality of a hard and bitter life, the peculiar institution of slavery, and the indignant anger of the owners and masters. Somerset Place shows the microcosm of the sad struggle that occurred before the partial emancipation of the Civil War. The large farm was owned by the scion of the Collins family that had founded the large farm decades before. Josiah Collins III and his wife Mary Riggs Collins came to the family plantation in 1830. Rather than an iron fist, he seemed to rule more with a gold plated hammer. He lived a lavish lifestyle, even using French as the household language for a time. He cleared the land with a harsh hand, growing corn that replaced the rice patties of years before. Collins and his overseer treated his slaves with typical cruelty, though his focus is sometimes placed on the fact that while he jammed his slaves in uncomfortable tiny quarters, he fed them adequately and provided a hospital for their care. He would have to, as the slaves did the unforgiving work of clearing the swampy land with canals and tree clearing. The canals would allow for the water to drain off well, providing adequate but not overwhelming moisture to the corn crops.

The canals would come back to haunt Collins, his wife, and ultimately, Somerset Place. Four children, two children of slaves, Zacharias Blount and Anderson Sawyer, and two children of Mr. and Mrs. Collins, Edward and Hugh, would be swimming in one of the canals when all would ultimately drown. Mary Collins would take this loss extremely hard, as would be expected. The family would ultimately lose three of their six children at too young an age.

It isn't the children that haunt the house, though. Mary Collins has been heard and felt in the house. Screams have been heard coming from the house, and cold spots have been felt in the grand plantation home. Locals have long heard the cries from Somerset. However, the state park employees are tight lipped about the events in the house. They normally do not talk about any haunting, focusing on the more provable realities of the plantation history.

In addition to the haunted house, the fields and slave houses are reportedly haunted. Mostly there are tales of a spiritual negative energy, more than ethereal figures. The general sadness of the life of a slave may be permanently imprinted on the land, with all the forced labor and loss churned into tearing the natural land away to create a farm.

Nearby to Somerset Place is Pettigrew State Park, a camping and day use area popular with campers and anglers. There is a path that connects the campsites with Somerset, allowing for a hike to the plantation. The more natural land is full of hard cypress trees, open at the trunks with notches big enough to stand in. The natural state seems to have happily taken in all the love that was drawn out from the plantation land. No ghosts haunt the trees, but sprites and strange lights have been spotted in the forests.

Somerset Place is open Tuesdays through Saturdays from 9 to 5. Tours are available during visiting hours. Camping is available at Pettigrew and visitors can walk over to Somerset via a short hiking trail.

Screaming Bridge

Williamston   35.76477° -77.00542°

Ghostly legends and haunting take all kinds of different forms. There is the truly strange haunting, where ghosts walk in the homes and places where they once walked in life. Then there are legends of spooky tales and chilling events that are popular tales but have little in common with real history. And finally, there's those wonderful urban legends, the tales told in middle schools and around campfires meant to scare kids and teenagers or dare them into a late night exploration out in the deep dark woods.

That's what the Screaming Bridge of Williamston has become.

The Screaming Bridge is a great lesson in urban legends. The effect, the end result, has always been the same. If a person goes out to the bridge at midnight, he will hear a woman screaming. Often there are attachments to the basic story. A pool of blood will appear on the road, people get scratches from an invisible assailant, a ghost may appear, but the idea is always the same. At midnight on the dark, silent road, a woman's cries will pierce through the inky night, a sound of fear and terror.

The cause of the screaming is the issue. Over time, the bridge has held the end of the legend while the beginning changes with the times. The most recent story takes in modern urban legends. A woman was coming back from a Halloween party, where she was dressed as a cat, complete with cat eye contact lenses. She had to pick up her baby from the sitters, and then when passing over the bridge, she couldn't see well due to the contacts. She crashed the car into the bridge and mother and child went over the edge. Both lost their lives in the icy water on the end of a cold October night.

Before this legend became popular, another tale was told in the 50s and 60s. The area was originally inhabited by the Yarrell family (the road, Yarrell Creek Rd., is named after them). One of the children of the family, a young girl, is said to have fallen into the creek and drowned. In more lurid tales, she dies a more tragic death, by murder or suicide. When people pass over the bridge, they can hear the sad moaning of the girl. On well moonlit nights, a girl can be seen sitting under a cypress, mourning her fate.

An even earlier tale that people heard from long ago was crueler and more murderous. The area originally was home to a mill run by the Yarrell family. Mr. Yarrell was a successful businessman, with a wife that he ultimately didn't like. Not wanting to share in his success, he tied his wife to a millstone and threw her, and it, over the old wooden bridge into the creek. Ever since, her screams from her horrific death can be heard under the bridge.

The bridge is just far enough off the beaten path for visitors to build up a proper scare as they head out to hear the screams. Halloween is a popular time to visit, and cars may be along the road in the dark as people drive up. It may also be hard to hear the screams, as sometimes they come from afar, when there are lots of people around. It's a dark and lonely road. Strangers of the mortal type may be more dangerous than the ghost under the bridge.

Attmore-Oliver House

New Bern   35.10828° -77.04227°

The lovely former Swiss colony of New Bern is one of the oldest settlements in North Carolina. History oozes from the homes and buildings of the town, from churches to businesses to private homes. The Attmore-Oliver House was built early in New Bern's history, constructed in 1790, and added to over the years. It is also considered one of the most haunted houses in New Bern.

The home was owned by the Attmore family, and by marriage the Oliver family, from 1834 until 1953, when the last members sold the home to the New Bern Historical Society. Over that time, the family saw a world pass by. One of the reasons surmised to cause the haunting is a plague of smallpox that caused the house to be quarantined for a time during the Civil War. Smallpox reared its ugly head as the Union occupation of the coastal towns could not handle the influx of different refugees from freed plantations as well as the flourishing ship trade. Smallpox and yellow fever rolled through the cities like a grimy and polluted wave, washing the diseases into the towns in a flood.

The ghosts of the Attmore-Oliver House may be a girl and a man. Actually, the ghosts may not be ghosts at all. It may be that poltergeists inhabit the house. A poltergeist is a "noisy ghost," and is known to move or throw objects in a location. People in the house have seen objects move or fly across the room. Guests have been pushed and pinched, and people have felt a tap upon their shoulders only to turn around and find nothing but empty space behind them.

The Attmore-Oliver House is now, and has been for a long time, the home to the New Bern Historical Society. The home is open for arranged tours, but has not shown much interest in doing paranormal investigations. However, they do open the house during October for a designed haunted evening, which is more performance than haunt. The house can be seen from the street, but it is on a main road, so walking by will get a better view than driving.

Bentonville Battlefield

Four Oaks 35.30221° -78.32213°

The Battle of Bentonville was the one of the last major battles of the Civil War, occurring in March of 1865, just before the surrender of General Lee's forces at Appomattox. The battles had become increasingly one sided, with Union General William Sherman having completed his destructive March to the Sea in order to crush the will and way for the Confederacy to fight. Sherman then planned to march through North Carolina and seize Raleigh. The remaining military strength in the South was commanded by General Joseph Johnston. His force, though underarmed compared to the Union forces, attempted to attack a split Union army and hopefully slow the inexorable attack of Sherman.

The battle lasted three days, from March 19 until the night of March 21, when Johnston retreated across the nearby Mill Creek. During the battle, the combined forces saw about 3,300 soldiers killed or wounded. The Union forces had taken over the local farming family's home, the Harper House, and used it as a makeshift hospital and triage. Soldiers were treated, with battlefield amputations common, in the ground floor of the house, while the Harper family, John and his wife Amy, along with their six children, were resigned to the top floor. Union and Confederate alike were treated, some well, some with contempt, along the house and yard. Most of the Confederate dead were buried in a mass grave near the Harper House, either after treatment at the home, or after being gathered from the battlefield.

The negative energy of the battle, soldiers on both sides knowing the battle was futile, that the war would be over soon, has leached itself out onto the land and the Harper House. The ghosts of six Union soldiers have been seen and felt on the grounds around the Harper House and visitor's center. The house itself has often been the site of strange lights, glowing orbs, and mysterious sounds. There are some claims that John Harper even still haunts his old house. He paces the place in an attempt to keep out the invading Union soldiers who littered his home and fields with blood.

The battlefield holds even more mystery. Visitors have heard the sounds of battle in the now peaceful land. Gunshots and artillery mix with the cries of the wounded and dying, even though the weapons of death have long since left the field.

One of the most intriguing stories of the haunted battlefield was told by Nancy Roberts in her book, *An Illustrated Guide To Ghosts*. She tells a story of Jim Weaver, a local hunter who was out on the night of the anniversary of the battle, March 19, 1905, who suddenly found himself in the middle of the battle between ghosts of both armies. The land had recited the memory of the terrible event, with spectral gray and blue clad soldiers sending forth death from their rifles, and, when close enough, from the melee of hand to hand combat. Jim witnessed a Yankee soldier attack a boy carrying the standard for a group of Confederate troops. Rooted to his spot in fear, he saw a rebel soldier come to the aid of his compatriot, only to receive a mortal wound from the Union soldier's bayonet. The Yankee then turned back to the young boy with the flag and stabbed him in the shoulder with a knife. The boy fell, his arm damaged. The ghostly battle then moved past Weaver into the darkness. Only when the fog of war faded was Weaver able to move again.

No one believed his story, of course. That is, not until he told his tale to a gathering of old Confederate veterans. Even then, the old soldiers took the story as more of a tall tale. They only one who did believe his account was a man who listened intently, while his arm hung useless in a sling. During the Battle of Bentonville, as only a 17 year old boy, he had taken a wound to the shoulder while carrying his line's standard. His brother had been killed trying to defend him.

Bentonville is a state historic site now. It is open Tuesday through Saturday from 9 to 5. Employees have been told to discourage discussion of ghosts and haunting, only talking about the historical aspects of the battlefield. Paranormal investigations are also discouraged, and after hours investigations are not advised. Trespassing is bad enough, but it can be more serious when it's on state property. There are re-enactments at the site where people get to spend the night on the grounds, and many re-enactors have seen something in their time on the battlefield.

Central

Cryptozoology and Paranormal Museum

Littleton   36.4271° -77.91355°

L ittleton is the home to the Cryptozoology and Paranormal Museum, a private collection focusing on the study of creatures not normally discussed in science. While the museum does include ghosts and haunting in its subjects, it has greatly embraced the study and discussion of Bigfoot sightings local to the state and area. Medoc Mountain, south of Littleton in nearby Hollister, seems to be a popular spot for the elusive creature. Mysterious sightings and telltale tracks have been found in the park.

In addition to their Sasquatch hunting, the museum also has a collection of haunted items, including a haunted doll collection. The star of this set is a Mrs. Beasley doll they acquired from a family who was all too happy to be rid of it. The family bought the doll, a toy that was a replica of the doll carried by the young girl Buffy in the TV show *Family Affair*, as a bit of nostalgia. The doll turned out to be a source of discomfort for the family. They would come home to find the doll no longer sitting as they left it, but turned around, or laying flat. After realizing that no one in the family was moving it, they decided it needed to go to a better home, and the Cryptozoology Museum was contacted. The doll now sits in a locked box, with a glass window for viewing. Various photographs of Mrs. Beasley show her in various different poses, even though she is locked behind glass. The doll apparently moved on her own.

Not that the house needed any help to be haunted and creepy. It was built in the 1850s, and people have known it was full of paranormal activity. Stephen Barcelo, a journalist for the Ney York *Daily News*, bought the house and moved down in 2014. Already an investigator of cryptids and strange creatures in New York, he became interested in the happenings in his new home town of Littleton. He turned the house into a museum in 2015, quickly becoming a major draw for visitors to the town. Barcelo reports of voices and full apparitions in the old house, along with confirming tales by his neighbors, who knew there was something otherworldly going on there.

There are multiple ghosts in the house. A young boy is still there. The child directed a clairvoyant to a section of a wall upstairs. Looking behind the tongue and groove wood, they found toys and blocks hidden in the old cotton batting. There are two women, a blonde and a brunette, who have appeared in the home, along with a man who shows up in the guest room, shaking the bed. Other shadowy figures appear as well.

It is no surprise that there are so many ghosts there. While some people may be lucky, or unlucky, enough to have one, this place has several. It is probably because the old house was used as a rooming house and brothel at different times. There are even hidden rooms in the old home.

Being interested, a de facto expert on the paranormal, Barcelo's museum has become a bit of a repository for weird stuff. In addition to the Mrs. Beasley doll, they received another doll, a clown, that was definitely creepy. It was even creepy in the way they got it. It was found hanging on a hook on the door. They got a different clown from a family that got it as a gift. The owner began having nightmares, and gave it to a daughter. She began having problems, too, and the thing was finally passed over to the museum.

What is it with clowns?!

If that wasn't creepy enough, Barcelo also has actual shrunken heads from Equador on display.

People who visit the museum have a change to take part both in a discussion on the paranormal, as well as learning more about the cryptozoological aspect of the area. Bigfoot sightings have been occurring in the county for a while, but only recently have been on the uptick. Logging in the area may be driving the timid creature out of its preferred habitat. A bigfoot type creature has even been seen nearby in a neighbor's back yard.

The Cryptozoology and Paranormal Museum is becoming a repository of new discoveries and reports of various cryptids across the state and region. They welcome people to file any discoveries, and have started a database for sharing information with other cryptid hunters. It also hosts tours with investigations in the house for visitors to participate. The museum is privately run. While there is no fee to visit, a donation certainly helps.

Mordecai House

Raleigh   35.79268° -78.63322°

G hosts can often be fickle creatures, going from playful to angry at any slight provocation, though the same thing can probably be said about mortals as well. Who knows how a ghost would feel if their name was pronounced wrong? Well, go to the Mordecai House in Raleigh and find out.

The Mordecai House is the oldest house in Raleigh still in its original location, and the home to what used to be the largest plantation in the county. The home is named for Moses Mordecai, who married into the family that built the house. Mordecai was a successful lawyer who came from a prominent Jewish family. His wife, Peggy Lane, came from an Episcopalian clan, and the marriage was not a happy one for the others in the Mordecai family. Moses would ultimately change the pronunciation of his name to the more southern Mor-duh-key.

The house stayed in the family until 1968, when the city of Raleigh bought the property. Local groups helped purchase the furniture to turn it into a museum and park for the city.

The house is haunted by a later descendant of Moses, Mary Willis Mordecai Turk. She has been seen and heard in the house over the years. A vaporous apparition appears in an old fashioned dress, a black skirt and white blouse, as her vision appears on the balcony or halls late into the evening. She has been heard playing the piano, and a gray mist has appeared over the instrument. Some workers and guides have even seen pictures move or come off the walls.

The house is open for tours, as is the rest of the park. The area is usually open from dawn to dusk, but the house can be seen from the street later in the evening, just in case Mary Willis is hanging out on the balcony.

Oakwood Cemetery

Raleigh   35.78604° -78.62757°

A cemetery full of life is the term used for Oakwood Cemetery. It was originally designed as a quiet resting place for the Confederate dead. The remains of a large number of soldiers were interred there in quick fashion after a threat from the occupying Federal officer stated that any Confederate not removed from the Rock Quarry Cemetery, where they planned to bury Union dead, would be cast into the streets to rot.

What started as a desperate race to rebury the dead has become a beautiful final backdrop of 102 acres for the dearly departed, holding numerous generals, soldiers, NC senators, and one very famous basketball coach.

The cemetery, with the sprawling tree lined paths, the old grave markers, and towering statues, is just aching to hold some ghosts. Investigators have found an abundance of orbs, and cold spots dot the land. Paranormal researchers believe that the cold spots are places where the ghosts attempt to manifest themselves, pulling the energy right out of the air to make something happen or for them to appear. There usually aren't any actual apparitions there, but the psychokinetic energy abounds in the expansive burial ground.

One legend that has been able to attach itself to the cemetery is a great urban legend. The Spinning Angel, also known as the Ratcliffe Angel, has gained a notoriety in the community. On Halloween, at midnight, the usually steadfast angel statue will lose her head and start spinning. Yes, the head is supposed to spin around on her neck twelve times at midnight on Halloween. Since this is so specific, and occurs only one time a year, the legend has grown to say that she will slowly spin around, the whole statue, if watched long enough. The statue is being a guardian of the cemetery, slowly looking all around to make sure her land is kept safe.

Of course, this story is really hokum, just a good tale to scare people or get them out late at night. The statue is as firm as carved stone can be. Sadly, some people don't believe this, and the angel has been damaged in the past.

Oakwood Cemetery is open to visitors, since it truly is a cemetery full of life. Walkers and joggers pass through the cemetery all the time. Tours are even available, in advance. They just ask that guests be respectful of the area and its denizens, including the ones at forever rest and the newly departed. Pictures of the statues are fine, just don't touch or stand on them. And no photographing funerals. People are welcome to visit, but must leave their pets at home, and the entire cemetery is smoke free.

Be aware that going at night, like at any cemetery, might attract attention from both the ghosts and the local police. The ghosts are said to scratch visitors, and, the police, well, this is in Raleigh, where Barney Fife comes to party. Behave well.

The Call of the Haunt

A Spooky Side Trip

I had the pleasure of taking up an acquaintance with several paranormal investigators as I wrote my books, including Eddie from NC HAGS, North Carolina Haints, Apparitions, Ghosts & Spirits. I took so much away from Eddie and his cohorts, all of it good. They may not have a TV show or get paid for what they do, but they are truly professional in every sense of the word. Diligent and skilled, yes, but what I liked most about talking with them was the kindness, honesty, and support that they gave when I discussed both my book and my subjects. For a group of people that delve deeply into the paranormal, they are truly very normal guys. This is just a little color on Eddie's take of what makes him want to investigate haunting.
-J.S.

Ghost Hunting was more than what I thought it would be. As a person that grew up with ghosts, I thought it would be interesting to find out what I had dealt with, all those years ago. In 2006 friends and I formed NC HAGS. Ours is a home grown group, with a plan to always report honestly what we find, and also try to figure out what or who we may capture in pictures, or on recorder. We feel we have done a very good job of staying true to our mission of honesty, and exploration.

With all that said, we had no clue as to the adventures this quest would lead us on. We have been all over North Carolina, and parts of Virginia on ghost hunts. It has been a fun, and sometimes scary journey. We have made new friends from every corner of the state. Fun, because of all the places, and access to places we have been granted while on hunts. Scary, because we didn't realize that some ghost wanted to scare us, or play tricks on us.

I have been sitting in an old house or building in the middle of nowhere, and suddenly realized someone or something is touching me, or making noise in the darkness. Bear in mind, we always know where each team member is at, so we don't spoil or contaminate evidence. So it really gets spooky, when you realize someone is there with you, but not a team member that you know. A good example is The Battleship North Carolina, in Wilmington, N.C. I can only say, I felt a heaviness surround my whole person in the medical area. This feeling stayed with me from 2 a.m. Until 6 a.m. when we left. It literally felt like the heaviness of a wet blanket was placed on me. Also, the feeling of dread.

Why do I still go hunting ghosts? I don't have ESP, or any otherworldly abilities. It's just, I love solving the mystery of possible ghosts in a specific area, or building. Also, I love meeting new friends. Some of these people have become close friends for life. You never know what you will find, unless you get out there and try.

Eddie (NC HAGS)

Clarksville Station

Roxboro   36.33739° -78.98311°

Clarksville Station is an old train depot that has more than the normal share of odd twists in its history. The Clarksville station isn't in Clarksville; it's not even in the right state. It has two train cars, but no railroad. And even though it's a station, it actually is a restaurant.

Clarksville Station used to serve the Atlantic and Danville Railroad, in Clarksville, Va., until it was closed down in 1973. The building, with its turn of the century style, was dismantled and moved into North Carolina and reassembled in Roxboro. It was turned into a restaurant, and two antique train cars were added to the place for a fitting bit of ambiance. It is the cars that have supplied a spooky addition to the restaurant.

The two cars were used in the Civil War to treat injured soldiers. One actually was a morgue car, where the bodies were stored. The other was used for surgery, such as it was in wartime, and treatment. Now guests to the restaurant can dine in the cars. The cars have both some sort of residual haunting, where employees have heard sounds of the past, the cries of the wounded, clanking sounds, mysterious noises coming from the train cars late at night even after the restaurant is closed. And the engineer of the train, a man in a suit and hat, has been seen in the cars. His visage has been known to appear in photographs and in a mirror.

Clarksville Station is open for lunch and dinner. No word on if they let ghost hunters in unless they are getting a bite to eat.

Gimghoul Castle

Chapel Hill

35.91196° -79.0361°

Spring in Chapel Hill warms the hearts of students attending the University of North Carolina as the days grow longer and brighter, with the vernal buds of pink, red, and white mixing with the Carolina Blue throughout the campus. Students who have focused on lessons now turn their eye to love.

But there is a dark corner of the land where the shadows grow long in the evening, and love becomes loss, and hope turns to troubles. The area of Piney Prospect is the home to both a gloomy, mysterious castle, and a terrible haunted legend.

In the spring of 1833, a freshman student named Peter Dromgoole had fallen for a beautiful young local girl named Fanny. Fanny was equally charmed by the young man from Virginia, and the two became a couple. They would often meet in the woods of Piney Prospect, near the campus, to sit on a large boulder while they spent time together, watching the sun filter through the tall trees, as the sun crept down and the shadows grew long. Evening would signal the time for Fanny to return home, and Peter to go back to his dormitory.

The two seemed to be a perfect couple, but there was another man who vied for Fanny's affections. A former friend of Peter's often attempted to flirt with the girl, and tormented Peter with thoughts of taking Fanny away. Peter attempted to avoid the other student, but he could not be avoided on the campus. After seeing the man talking to Fanny, Peter finally became enraged, and attacked his former friend. After the two were pulled apart, a duel was challenged, and accepted before the glove had symbolically hit the ground.

The two, with their seconds in tow, met at Piney Prospect. The land was isolated, far enough away that the professors and deans from the campus would not know of what happened there. Pistols, heavy curved flintlocks, were loaded for the two men. Peter and his rival stood back to back, and quietly paced off the requisite ten steps in the soft loam of the woods. They turned, lowering the ungainly pistols upon each other. The heavy triggers were squeezed, trembling hands delivering death through the weapons. The locks snapped, sparking a powder that would flare and smoke, igniting the charge that would propel a lead ball out of the pistols. One slug would fly free, whipping through the woods, snapping through leaf and branch with unconcerned ease. The other would race to its mark, cracking through bone and flesh. Peter Dromgoole would see his life pour out in a sanguine river from a wound in his chest. He would stagger and fall, lurching over the very rock he had sat with Fanny. His blood would gush out where his heart had done the same in the days and weeks before.

Horrified, the remaining three men had finally realized the nature of their deed, as Peter Dromgoole's corpse lay bleeding out over a moss covered rock in the middle of the forest. They hastily dug under the rock with their hands until they had a makeshift grave, where they cast the bloodied mortal remains of young Peter. As the shadows crept up from the trees, the students covered the body. Their crime covered, they swore a quiet oath to each other never to reveal what they had done.

Little did they know that one more person was aware of the gory event. Peter Dromgoole, even after death, would tell of what happened to him, and in more than one way. Peter's parents would receive a letter soon after the event, from Peter, saying that they may hear of something terrible happening to him, and that he was sorry for the shame and sadness he caused.

Peter would reveal his death in another way, too. The other three students who took part in the duel spread the rumor that Peter had left to join the army, abandoning his studies for a life in the military. Fanny was surprised that her love would leave without telling her, or discussing his plans in any way. She went up to their favorite spot, in Piney Prospect, to sit on the rock where they used to spend their days together. Little did she know that the sticky sap on the stone was Peter's drying blood. And that the rock was actually his tomb. Fanny would sit and wait. Then, when the sun set through the trees, she saw Peter. He walked through the woods from campus, as he always did, but before reaching the clearing and his love, he disappeared into the mist.

Fanny realized that Peter had died, but never knew how. She often would go back to Piney Prospect to wait for Peter, in hopes that his spirit would reach her, but it never would.

The tale of Peter Dromgoole would go on to become a legend in the UNC campus. In 1889, a secret society would be founded under Peter's name, the Order of the Dromgoole. William Davies, one of the founders, changed the name to the Order of the Gimghoul, "in accord with midnight and graves and weirdness." The property where Peter's rock and his grave sat was bought by the order, and in 1926 a castle was constructed on the land. Originally named Hippol Caslte, the building became known as Gimghoul. The rock is still front and center for the castle, and the blood remains there, never to be removed.

The castle and its order are private, secretive, and visitors are far from welcome. Interlopers into the castle will be prosecuted.

However, the castle and rock are still on a public road. Piney Prospect is popular with people out for a walk or run, and explorers can easily drive up the gravel road. Driving up in the twilight or during a spring thunderstorm will enhance the eerie feeling.

Carolina Inn

Chapel Hill   35.90958° -79.05464°

When someone checks into a fine hotel, there always is that one fleeting moment where thoughts turn to how to stay there forever. How can you move into a fancy place, get clean sheets every day, no worries, no power bills, no repairs to do, and just walk down to the restaurant whenever you get hungry? The notion passes quickly when the math and the finances are considered. It would be far too difficult to stay in a hotel forever.

Unless you are a ghost.

The Carolina Inn is said to be haunted by as many as 20 ghosts throughout the sprawling Georgian style hotel. The inn was built in the 1920s as a place for visiting professors and alumni to stay in elegance while visiting the campus. The most noticeable spirit is that of a doctor who actually figured out how to live in a fine hotel. Dr. William Jacocks was a graduate of UNC-Chapel Hill, with a medical degree to complement his many other undergraduate studies. He spent his years improving the health of both his home state as well as traveling to Dehli, India to treat tropical diseases. He retired, if that term could be used for a man who always remained in fine health, in 1948, in Chapel Hill, where he moved in permanently to the Carolina Inn. Jacocks called Room 252 home for 17 years, until near his death in 1965. Since he seemed to like staying there so much, he still calls the inn his home.

Now, Room 252 is part of several remodeled rooms at the inn, and his room is currently considered to be 256, though it exists in the layout of four rooms. The main room, 256, would lock on its own, necessitating an entry through the window to get the door open.

Electronic locks were added, but even afterward, the doors would still close and lock without reason on occasion. Jacocks interacts in the room in various ways. He will open curtains, move bath mats and rugs, and often leave a mysterious scent of flowers.

Not only have Jacocks' actions been documented, his ghost appears in the inn on occasion. A well dressed man walks the halls, often checking the doors to see if he can find an open room.

Paranormal investigators have found evidence of a presence in Jacocks' room, but also detected at least one other person there. The sound of a piano playing has been both heard and recorded, even late at night when no music is played. Ghostly activity has been seen and felt throughout the inn.

The Carolina Inn happily embraces the haunted legends it has. It even offers a package deal for Dr. Jacocks' room. Halloween is a fun time around the campus, and if alums want to have a more sedate time than running around Franklin Street in costume, they can stay at the Carolina Inn for a truly haunted night. The inn is known as the university's living room, but staying there isn't cheap, especially when the Tar Heels are playing a game. Reservations need to be made in advance, since the inn could fill up, and some of the guests may not want to leave.

Seven Hearths

Hillsborough   36.07554° -79.09658°

The Seven Hearths house, just off the main street of sleepy little Hillsborough, is a warm and inviting old home that was built in 1754. The building was first owned by William Reed, who was both the high sheriff of Orange, as well as a tavern owner. The building probably was a tavern at two different times in its existence. The original home had additions over the centuries, and became famous for having seven fireplaces, thus the name Seven Hearths.

With the house being so old, and so much history, it would be little surprise to find that the place is haunted. The house is not haunted by a famous person, like one time owner and writer Peter Taylor, or an unknown denizen of the tavern, but a couple of family members. The Hayes family owned the house through its descendants for over 150 years. A daughter, Jane Hayes, died from tuberculosis at the age of 16, and her youthful spirit never left the home. Owners have seen a ghostly figure of a young blonde girl in a nightgown walk from room to room. There are tales that she has been seen staring out the window down toward the street below.

An additional ghost, and an odd one at that, is that of Dr. William Hayes, who lived in the house up into the 1920s. He was a spiritualist, searching for the messages of life after death. In a way, he may have found it, but he may also be regretting it. Dr. Hayes has been seen in the house, but in the form of a cat. Only the cat has Dr. Hayes' head.

Seven Hearths is still a private home. It is a historic house, and because of that, visitors are expected to view it often, from the street or sidewalk. Hillsborough is a nice small town, with lots of walking trails, and shops to visit, so it is easy to take a stroll down to the home. Just don't go in. The cat thing would keep most people out.

Stewartsville Cemetery

Laurinburg   34.73844° -79.41307°

Laurinburg is already home to a rather mysterious spot in the strange and mysterious gravity hill that sits at the end of Stewartsville Cemetery Rd. It may be at the end, but any driver stopping there and putting the car into neutral will find their trip beginning again as the car starts to coast back up the hill the way they came. It's unlikely the car will coast several miles back, but if the driver turns around, they will pass the namesake Stewartsville Cemetery, a bone orchard with residents having some unique stories, as well as some rather ghostly happenings.

Stewartsville Cemetery is an old cemetery. It has a rather interesting mixture of inclusiveness and segregation. The graveyard holds both black, white, and Native American remains all in the same piece of land. However, each is separated into sections. A chain link fence separates the black and white graves, while a low set of concrete posts delineates the graves of the natives to the land.

Permanent residents include Lauchlin McLaurin, the founder of Laurinburg. The poor guy founded the town, then got struck by lightning. Congressman James Stewart was also buried there. Colin Lindsay rests in the cemetery. His life was colorful, as he was a serious and vitriolic preacher in the town. His birth was also just as colorful. He was known as the person born after his mother was buried. Long before he was born, his mother, still in Scotland, went into a deep coma. Thinking she was dead, the family buried her. Wanting to take advantage of the soft earth, her grave was uncovered by robbers after her wedding ring. As they began to cut her finger for the ring, she awoke, startling the thieves. Six years later, a healthy mom gave birth to Colin, who later immigrated to North Carolina.

Curiously, there is no specific ghost story attached to the graveyard. The legends that have grown out of the area are more because of the wildness of the land, and the people that were buried there. Supposedly, the spirits that reside there in death were not so good in life. The ghosts are from some rather nasty or at least restless souls that can't go one way and don't want to go the other. After midnight, the ghosts get restless and walk the graveyard, trying to find a way to cross out of the property. Unfortunately for them, they are trapped by the confines of the cemetery. They try to escape, but must return to their grave before sunrise.

The cemetery can be seen from the road, and is off limits to visitors at night. Considering the alleged unhappy nature of the ghosts there, it may be for the best not to run into one late at night.

Devil's Tramping Ground

Harper's   Crossroads
35.58478° -79.48664°

Even though the Devil's Tramping Ground is a place devoid of life, a circle in which nothing will grow, it sure has a lustrous patina to the age old legendary place. Everyone in the state knew of the Devil's Tramping Ground, as much as they knew of the mysterious hoofprints at Bath, or the legend of Blackbeard. The Devil's Tramping ground was ingrained nostalgia for kid and adult to know about the circle of death, where the devil paces each night.

Out beyond Siler City, it itself a place steeped in NC lore as being oft mentioned by Andy Taylor and others of Mayberry on The Andy Griffith Show, is a tiny patch of dead earth. It is circular, small, about maybe 20 or 30 feet across. Nothing grows there. Even though it is surrounded by forest, no seed has ever taken hold in this small patch of ground.

Legend says that the devil himself comes out at night there, and paces in an endless circle, plotting his nefarious deeds. No item left inside will remain for long. Old Pitch, when pitching a fit, will kick anything out of his way. Any type of plant life will find no root, as the devil's hoof, smoking with brimstone, has long since sapped the life out of the land. Even campers, if they dare spend the night there, will find themselves moved out of the circle, even just barely, by the time they wake up in the morning.

The Devil's Tramping Ground has changed a bit since it was made famous in the 1950s with articles and books on the haunted lands of North Carolina. The other trees grow taller now, and make the circle seem smaller. The detritus of hundreds of years of fallen limbs can litter the place. Still, no plant will grow there. It is still a circle, albeit different looking than the old sandy patch from long ago.

In reality, the Devil's Tramping Ground probably has a more mundane reason for being. Or a differently supernatural one. It has been long known that the place exists, for more than 300 years. Ideas circulated include it being an old natural salt lick for animals that was worn into the ground, or the site for a press where mules walked in endless circles driving a machine. Another premise is that it is the preserved ground for Chief Croatan, a tribal leader who fell in the area during a battle. It could also be the home of an ancient UFO landing or a strange vortex.

Whatever it is, it's there, and has been a famous stopping point for ages. No ghosts, though there may be something to those legends about things moving out of the circle. There's an easy pull off nearby, and a short path into the woods. Beware that some people have taken to camping and partying there, starting fires, which definitely has lead to a lack of plant life. Steer clear of any questionable people, and maybe take a garbage bag to clean up around the edges.

Carolina Theater

Greensboro   36.06969° -79.79184°

If a theater opened its doors for the first time on Halloween night, it certainly would need a ghost to help in the celebrations. The Carolina Theater is fortunate to have three or four.

Perhaps it would be better to say it is fortunate to have several, but one of the ghosts is quite unfortunate.

Opened on Halloween night in 1927, the Carolina Theater in Greensboro was a extravagant center of entertainment in the city. It hosted vaudeville acts, plays, concerts, and films over the years. But before it was built, a home was on the property. The first ghost of the theater is a young boy who sadly died at his home. Now his spirit plays little pranks in the theater, moving things and throwing items onto the stage.

The theater is also haunted by a worker who died during construction. He is seen in worker's clothes walking through the usually empty theater. He is most likely a steelworker that died from a fall when working on the theater. He has been seen but does not interact with people in the building.

During a practice of *A Streetcar Named Desire* in the 1970s, a woman in pink, with a pillbox hat, was seated in the balcony watching the rehearsal. The actors thought nothing of it, until she arose and walked away, right through the wall.

The last ghost, and most famous, has an even more tragic story. In 1981, Melvalina Ferguson came in to watch a movie. Little would anyone know that Melvalina, a homeless woman in medical need, would be refused her medicine that day. She vowed that Greensboro would burn that night. After the movie, she hid behind the seats. When everyone left, she went into the south stairwell and set fire to rolls of polyester fabric which had been gifted to the theater by Guilford Mills. Melvalina removed her clothes down to her slip, and let the fire take her. The damage to the Carolina was extensive and it took a year to repair the damage. If not for one fireproof door, the theater would have been lost.

Melvalina died in the fire, sadly possessed by her own ghosts and demons, but her spirit seems to have found a home in the theater. She has been seen, a floating apparition, a lady in white, just her slip, surrounded by a surreal glow. She, too, appears in the balcony. Once spotted, she lingers for a few moments, only to vanish into the air. She doesn't seem to interact with anyone, but she does not seem to be malevolent, either. Perhaps she found a bit of peace at her death, and her ethereal remains are content to haunt the theater quietly.

Today the Carolina Theater is home to concerts, live theater, classic and independent films, and also a source for local performances as well in their third floor theater, The Crown. That area which was the balcony has been sealed off from the main theater and turned into a more intimate setting. The Carolina Theater is open to ticket holders for their shows, but many actors and workers seem happy to discuss their experiences there. Even if a ghost doesn't show up, a good performance is guaranteed.

Lydia's Ghost

Jamestown   35.99687° -79.92601°

It is a dark and lonely night that finds a car's headlights trying to pierce the gloom of black along the old roads of Jamestown. Even the air seems weary, as it lets out a fine rain in fits and spurts. The driver flicks his wipers on and off, just smearing the water across his windshield. It does little good. Nothing cuts the murkiness of the evening. He slows, knowing the road to be curved, narrow, and slick. Accidents have happened before.

His high beams shine on the upcoming underpass, an old concrete obstacle to the cars that pass under the rail line that rises above the constricted road. There, in the dark, stands a woman, dressed in white, a fancy dress that seems both new and old at the same time. She has a worried look on her face. This is a terrible place to be standing on a rainy night, thinks the driver as he slows. Gallant, but humble and compassionate, he offers the girl a ride.

"Can you take me to High Point? I'm trying to get home," she says. She will say little else, except a vague address that the young man, a High Point local himself, knows somewhat. He turns up the heat to dry the poor girl, and offers her his sweater. She needs it more than him, he thinks.

He asks how she got there, how she was stranded at the old underpass so late at night. She reveals little. "My name is Lydia, "she responds, in s strained whisper. "I was at a dance in Raleigh. My boyfriend and I got into a fight. He.. he let me out..."

Wanting to know more, to understand how something like that could happen to the quiet and sweet girl in his car, he pressed on, but Lydia responds, "Why so many questions? Questions don't matter now. Now that I'm going home." She will say no more, and the two drive in relative silence.

Arriving at her home, the young man will stop the engine, then get out to go open her door. As he comes around, in the dim mist of the fog in his headlights, he discovers she is gone. No sound of the door slamming gave away her exit. There was no ruffle of feminine lace and soft cotton from her white dress. She seemed to have disappeared.

Curious, and concerned, the man goes to the door and knocks. Not Lydia, but still, someone like her, he thinks... her mother. Same visage, same haunted, sad look in her eyes. "Did Lydia come in? Is she alright?" he asks.

The woman is aghast. Her weary frame draws up, little strength in her body. Is this some kind of sick joke? She berates the man for being so cruel. But he doesn't understand. "I just... I just gave her a ride home. I found her at the old underpass in the rain. I just wanted to make sure she was alright." His earnest plea of compassion softens and tames the old woman. She explains it to the boy.

"That was my daughter, Lydia. She was killed at that curve in a car accident coming home from a dance. I think she's just trying to get back home."

Thus ends the tale, but the legend of Lydia lives on to this day. The story dates back to as early as 1924, and has been carried on in campfire tales and urban legends ever since. Lydia has been seen by motorists for decades. Children have hung their mothers' slips on coathangers by the underpass on Halloween. Even Lydia's death certificate has been hunted down, never revealing her last name or her mother's address. Even now, as the old road has been moved, and a newer underpass was built, it is believed that Lydia's ghost walks the road, still looking for a way to get home.

Little Red Man

Winston-Salem   36.08728° -80.24215°

One of the most well told and well liked ghost legends of North Carolina comes from Old Salem and the Moravians that flourished there. The Little Red Man story has been told and written about in so many ghost books of the Old North State that it is a staple of the historical spiritual record. It could be because it mixes so many things into the story, loss and kindness, playfulness and spookiness, absolute assuredness of a haunting with the absolutely sure riddance of the ghost. It is a tale that knows no season.

The tale of the Little Red Man in Old Salem is printed in almost every book that tells of North Carolina ghosts. The simple story is well known, but with little detail to flesh out the happenings and causes of the haunting. Most know of Andreas Kresmer, a member of the Moravians, dying and haunting the Single Brothers dwelling for a time, with his distinguishable red cap ever present on the ghost's head. Little more is ever said, outside of numerous sightings over the years. Time has a way of turning history into myth, and the story holds a lot more than just this simple tale.

Andreas Kresmer was born in Pennsylvania in 1753, and moved to North Carolina in 1766, where he became a shoemaker. He would settle into the Moravian Wachovia tract of Salem at only 18, in early 1772. There he would be by all accounts a kind and diligent young man, a true partner in the community. It would be of little surprise that he was one the men working on a new cellar for the Single Brothers Quarters late at night on March 25, 1786.

The Moravians had found that, generally, an easy way to excavate the soil was to dig out from underneath, creating an open spot on the bottom of the earth, then carefully use the weight of the soil to help break it down, then remove the excess. Several of the Bretheren had expressed concern for this method on their current excavation, as the soil was loose, and seemed to be coming down of its own accord. Furthermore, Kresmer was a small man, and also was warned by others not to kneel at the base of the loamy cliff. While no one should have been close to the base and its impending danger, being on his knees only meant it would be easier to cover Kresmer if the earthen wall should give way.

Sadly, this is exactly what happened late that night. Another man, Joseph Dixon, was covered up to his shoulders. Kresmer was nowhere to be seen. Working furiously, the Bretheren were able to dig out the two men. Dixon was uninjured but Kresmer had been buried alive. As per the usual procedures of the time, both men were bled, a small cut to see how their blood flowed. Dixon had regular, typical blood flow, while Kresmer, who complained of pain, had little pressure, indicating a probable internal injury. His left leg had also been broken.

The congregation was able to gather and say their farewells to the kind little man who was part of them. Andreas Kresmer died quietly at 2 am the following morning, after receiving the blessing from his congregation.

Kresmer was buried two days later in the Moravian burial ground, known as God's Acre, following the simple tradition of the Moravian church, with a small recumbent headstone that show that all are equal in God's view.

While Kresmer's body was quickly laid to rest, his spirit, in one way or another, stayed restless. Kresmer was known to be a playful, fun sort. He was also known by his occupation of shoemaker, often carrying a small hammer. Soon after his death, the sounds of tapping could be heard in the Single Brothers House. Residents would jokingly remark, "Oh, that's just Brother Kresmer!" But when the sounds kept happening, without reason or explanation, the more ghostly explanation began to take hold. Later, the sound of light footfalls could be heard in hallways, though no man walked them.

Later, Kresmer himself would be seen. A small man would appear, always clad in a red cap, sometimes mentioned as a red jacket, often seen in the darkened hallways of the house. When chased, he would playfully get away, never caught, never caught up. His figure became a somewhat regular visage, with several reports of its sighting. One of the most famous tales happened much later in the history of Salem.

The Single Brothers House changed its mission and became a home for elderly women after a time. This was when one of the more famous sightings occurred. The tale goes of "Little Betsy," the granddaughter of a resident, who would often go to visit her grandmother. Betsy had been stricken deaf as an infant, and was only learning to talk as she got older. Because of her hearing loss, she knew nothing about legends and tales, never hearing the stories from her elders or her friends. She probably did not even know what a ghost was, let alone know that the building was haunted by Kresmer. One day when visiting, Betsy had been playing around the building. She then went to her grandmother and asked who the little man in the red cap was that waved for her to come and play. Betsy's tale became the most famous documented sighting of Kresmer in the building.

Other sighting would come and go, only the famous ones, or the ones with a good story attached, seemed to live on. The Little Red

Man appeared for decades. His final appearances also seemed to be the ones that drove him out. A visitor to Old Salem, often referred as "a prominent citizen," would have the fortune, maybe dubious in his eyes, to spy Kresmer. He gave chase but never caught the playful spirit. While residents put up with Kresmer's antics, and seemed to even delight in them, putting shame to a high up muckity muck in the city was too much to bear. A minister was brought in to perform some form of exorcism. Kresmer, the Little Red Man, was ordered to rest, that his time on earth was well and truly done. He never appeared again after that.

Today the Single Brothers House can be toured as part of the Old Salem tour. Visitors should note that the house was built in two sections. The older part is a mix of brick and timber frame, built in 1769, while the newer, by only seventeen years, is all brick. Since Kresmer was evicted from his haunted abode, there really is no chance of seeing him, but the tour is fun anyway.

Randolph Mine

Gold Hill 35.51277° -80.34392°

The first gold discovery in the United States occurred in North Carolina, at the farm home of a German illegal immigrant, John Reed, who defected from the British Army and settled in Cabarrus County to raise a farm and a family. His son found a large and attractive stone in the dried river bed of Reed's farm, which they used for several years as a door stop. It took a few years to discover what they had, and to begin to collect the valuable metal, but soon enough, John Reed and his family began to pull in gold from his rapidly growing lands.

While John Reed never let the money he made affect him, the rest of the area was hit with a disease desired and dreaded, gold fever. In nearby Rowan County, the town of Gold Hill sprung out of the mines, sprouting the predictable growth for the needs of hard men doing a hard job. Gold Hill became the envy of tiny Charlotte, with the future Queen City's mayor once commenting on his wish that Charlotte could only be as prosperous as Gold Hill. With 29 saloons along its main street, as well as the requisite brothels that accompanied the drinking establishments, the town ballooned into a population of up to 5,000 men, with their accompanied families, wives and children, alongside. The mines were hard work, and paid well, about twice the average pay of most any other job. However, conditions were horrendous. Death hid in every darkened nook of the mines. And what didn't get the workers down below in the mine shafts would often attack them above the ground. Disease was rampant, with that many people in such a small area, and little to no medical care. If the mine didn't kill a man, and disease couldn't find purchase, well, there was always... murder.

Gold Hill is the home to several ghosts, especially at the old Randolph Mine shaft, where several people died in the 850 feet deep shaft. One mysterious death is that of Aaron Klein. Klein had come to Gold Hill like all the other miners to dig for gold and make some money. The only difference he had from the other men was the root of his last name. Klein was teased and tormented by the hateful words of anti-Semitic miners. Perhaps another difference that Klein had was that while he came to dig for gold, he also fell in love. Elizabeth Moyle was the daughter of a mine manager; the two would become engaged and began to plan for their marriage. With the scarcity of women in general to the mines and area, this rubbed many of the other miners the wrong way. Only Stan Cukla was the one to actually voice his hatred and judgment on their upcoming nuptials. It was soon after that Klein's pet dog, a little puppy really, was found killed at the entrance to the shaft. Klein was nowhere to be seen, and was thought to have been run off.

It was only days after Klein's disappearance that a strange shimmering began to appear at the entrance to the mine. Several miners soon supposed the specter to be that of a deceased Aaron Klein. As more and more people talked of it, most still thinking that it may be a natural phenomenon, Cukla became only more agitated. He began talking to himself, muttering about Klein and the ghost. He would be seen at the bottom of the Randolph shaft, stumbling in the darkness of the 850 foot pit, tripping over the rubble that fell there. He was seen there one night, but was never seen coming back up during the day.

The next morning, his body was found on top of the jagged spoil, lifeless and broken, pummeled into a nearly unrecognizable mess. It was later surmised that Cukla had killed Klein, thrown his body down the shaft, and in his fear of the unrelenting haunting from Klein's ghost, went down into the hellish pit to find Klein's remains. Instead he met his grisly and well deserved end at the hands of the ghost of Aaron Klein.

The tale goes on to say that Elizabeth, saddened by her loss, never married. He spirit is said to walk the lake nearby the shaft. Aaron Klein and his puppy have also been known to walk the pond.

There are certainly other ghosts that haunt the mines or walk the town of Gold Hill. Considering the number of unforeseen deaths, the only issue might be determining who it was that died, more than if a ghost exists. There are numerous stories of a disembodied figure, a ghost in pieces, that haunts several spots along the gold trail in the town. One story tells of Joe Newman, a part owner in one of the mines, along with his brother, Walter. Walter, in an attempt to cut Joe out of the business, set dynamite under Joe's house, blowing his brother to smithereens. Joe's head, separate from his arms, torso, and legs, floated around the Randolph mine. Curiously, after Walter died, he was spotted walking the darkened streets of Gold Hill. One ghost was doomed by murder, the other cursed by it.

A similar story, but at a different location, is told of the powder house, a storage facility built away from the rest of the mines. The old powder house was used to store explosives, dynamite, that was used in opening the caves for mining. The powder house was a dark structure, dug into a hillside, so that if any explosion happened, the earth would dampen the blast, and the mines would not be threatened by the shock. Well, two men went into the powder room in order to get some dynamite from a storage crate. In order to open the box, one of them hit the crate with a pick. The impact was strong enough to not only open the crate, but open the man's chest to the business end of his pickaxe he had used when the dynamite was set off accidentally. The other man was blown from the room, but miraculously survived. The hapless pickaxe wielder probably did not live long enough to discover his pick had become embedded in his chest, as he was blown apart by the explosion.

In more recent times, strange lights and a truly disembodied apparition have appeared in the old powder house. The tale is similar to Joe Newman's in that it appears as only parts of a body, not the whole figure. Most figure this to be the unknown man who was blown to bits in the powder house.

These are just a few of the old ghost tales of old Gold Hill. The place is so full of death, strife, and tragedy, that it is amazing that the ghosts don't walk by day as well, sharing the town with the new guests, visitors and tourists to the quaint village. The woods may have darker, older spirits, people or animals that lived long ago, and never truly left the memory of the land. Gold Hill shines today like the precious metal after which it was named, but now it gleams with a more historic radiance of time gone by. Only when it gets dark in the sky does the darker side of the old town come out to mix with the living.

Blakeney House

Monroe   34.98044° -80.54142°

It's been a home, a restaurant, and now a mission training and bible study business. It was haunted, possibly by three ghosts. It's not haunted anymore, but not for the reasons most would think.

Built in 1903, the William Blakeney house was built for a wealthy yet miserly man who was rumored to have stored money in hiding places all over his new home. Blakeney, a noted banker of the town, was extremely wealthy. Tales say he was either followed home after removing money from his bank during the beginnings of the Depression, or he died in a car accident. Either way, his death was tragic. His ghost has been seen in the house by locals and residents over the years since.

There is also the ghost of a little girl, often seen staring out an upstairs window. The little bit of legend attached to her is that she witnessed her parents killed in a car accident from the window, and continues to stare out, even after her own passing.

Another ghost haunts the building, a lady, or a young girl, in red.

Most of the tales center around the happenings inside the house. Blakeney has been seen, but he never communicates with the living. The girl in red is said to have been so vivid that she passes for a living person, talking with others before disappearing into the ether. While the usual door slamming and unearthly footsteps have been heard, there are a few odd and unique events in the building. After being sold, the house turned into a restaurant, with a private upstairs dining area. Once set up for a formal event, the room was closed and sealed so no one would mess up the fancy place settings. After a huge crash was heard, staff went up to find the entire upstairs was messed up, plates and silverware everywhere. Another rather interesting tale is that candles had been known to light themselves. It might be easy to explain how a cold draft would blow out a candle, but to light them on their own adds to a truly spooky experience.

Unfortunately, the place is no longer haunted. No, the ghosts didn't leave. The building is now used as a bible study and mission preparation business. The owners and workers there say nothing like that ever happens, and the stories are not true. Were the stories just made up and later embellished by the locals? Were the ghosts run out finally? Or do the current residents just think that the weird sounds are just the weird sounds of an old house? Only the ghosts will know that.

McGlohon Theater

Charlotte   35.22913° -80.8401°

Charlotte, with its gleaming skyline, rich with the wealth of big banking, its successful pro sports franchises, home of high speed NASCAR racing, as well as the myriad museums that dot the urban cityscape, seems unlikely a place for the dead, new or ancient, to wander far from their graves. Surely the beacon of big city life for North Carolina is so lively that there cannot be ghosts residing in the Queen City.

But Charlotte, like all of the Tar Heel State, is a haunted land.

The McGlohon Theater is just a small part of a bigger ghostly network, but the ghosts are well known to the visitors and staff of the theater. It originally was the First Baptist Church in Charlotte, built in 1908. By the 1970s, the church no longer used the property and it was sold to the city in 1977. It was refurbished and became a jewel in the crown of the Queen City as the McGlohon Theater, named after jazz pianist, songwriter, and Charlotte favorite son Loonis McGlohon.

Once it became a theater, workers soon discovered the place was probably haunted. When in the basement, a singer could be heard above them, performing a gauzy and vague gospel. Empty hallways are filled with the tread of phantom footsteps, the sounds of souls who walked the building long ago, even when the theater is mostly vacant.

Since the ghosts were only discovered once the building was converted into a theater, it is assumed that the ghosts come from the building's church days. Indeed, with the dome and stained glass still remaining, it very well may be that the souls still visit their house of worship. Curiously, the redeveloped area has a rather apropos name, Spirit Square.

Founders Hall

Charlotte   35.2271° -80.84245°

The city center of Charlotte is dominated by a giant skyscraper of the Bank of America Corporate Center, home to the largest bank in the U.S. In addition to the towering modern gold mine for the Queen City, the building and surrounding structures are home to shopping, art centers, bookstores, and coffee houses. The modern version of Founders Hall has everything a fast paced urbanite on the go would need.

Yet, oddly enough, long ago the needs of the people at Founders Hall included a dead body, fresh if possible.

In the 1800s, the area of Founders Hall was home to a medical school, and the medical school would pay good money for a cadaver for its students to perform autopsies on. Students were sometimes expected to get their own dead bodies, and usually there were no questions asked about where it came from.

In order to get a cadaver, grave snatchers would keep an ear out for the newly passed. Otherwise healthy people, hopefully not damaged, not decrepit, were preferred. The bodies had to be gotten soon after burial, too. Sometimes even within the night of the funeral. The ground would be soft, the body not yet begun to decay.

So it was done one night that when a poor girl in nearby Salisbury passed away, her body was unceremoniously removed from the freshly dug grave in the dark of the night. Her final resting place became not so final as the soft earth was quickly removed from above her wooden coffin. There was no time to cover their marks, and the grave robbers left without even filling in the hole left so empty.

Her corpse was delivered to the medical school that morning, and an autopsy was performed. Without care or refrigeration, the body's remains wouldn't last long. What did last was the restless spirit of a young girl both taken too soon in life, then taken from her grave in death. Her spirit wandered the halls, moaning and screaming in torment. She had been seen pleading with people, telling them of her plight. The happenings became so regular that ultimately the local police were involved, and tried to find what little remains they could to return them to her grave. It seemed to do little good, as the screaming continued, with doors slamming or opening.

Even today, people who work in Founder's Hall still say they have heard the moaning of the girl, a sad sound of a child left in between two worlds. The large new buildings may be a labyrinth for the spirit of a girl who barely had a chance to grow up in tiny Salisbury in the 1800s. It probably would be difficult even in today's time to determine exactly where she haunts Founders Hall.

Old St. Paul's Church

Newton   35.67773° -81.24336°

Early churches, especially small town churches, were not built with much flashy style on the outside of them. Mostly they were made to keep the winter outside and only let in the good portion of the summer. Old St. Paul's Evangelical Lutheran Church would be a prime example of that. Plain white, with two stories and a slanted roof, it looks more like a house drawn by a child than any modern idea of a church. Without the sign and roadside marker identifying the house of worship, and perhaps the acre left for God in the form of a cemetery, no one would recognize this as a church. There isn't even a steeple or cross upon the building.

But inside, now there was a place built for worship. Built in 1820 by 18 year old Henry Cline out of hand hewn wood, he put his effort into the interior. The church has a balcony as well as main floor. With it being built in the early 1800s, there had to be room for the segregation of slaves of the parishioners. The balcony was built for the slaves, a few rows of narrow benches where they could look down upon the pastor, preaching on a raised pulpit. The balcony was reached by a narrow twisted staircase from the ground floor. The separation continued on the ground level. The women sat on a different side than the men, with open pews so that their long dresses would fit in the seat rows. The pews also had foot rails so that mothers could put their feet up and hold small children more easily.

The ghostly legend that accompanies this church is both sad and gruesome. In 1861, a local landowner named Colonel Hildebran had tracked one of his slaves that had escaped the colonel's imprisonment to the church. With the same amount of compassion for human life that he had for sanctity of a house of worship, the colonel gunned down the poor slave who was hiding in the balcony of the church. Bloodstains and a handprint were left in the wood from where the murdered man fell.

Today, the bloodstains are still there, never able to be cleaned or removed. The ghost of the slain slave still haunts the old church, no longer used for services. On rare occasions, the organ to the church can be heard playing even though no fingers touch the keys.

Sally's Bridge

Lincolnton   35.43269° -81.17219°

Visiting this narrow bridge, all alone, late at night, one might actually start to believe that this story is true.

Poor Sally was stood up by her prom date. Rather than go the prom alone and face the shame of not having a date, she decided instead to drive herself home. Distressed and weeping, she drove down the narrow gravel path of Will Schronce Road in the darkening evening. Blinded by her tears, she misjudged the edge of the one lane bridge and crashed over it, plunging down into the creek. In the darkness, alone, Sally passed away, but not on.

From then on, people would say that they could visit the bridge, calling out to Sally, and that she would appear, walking up to them, up the embankment from the river, only to vanish once she set foot upon the road.

The legend lived on to become a tale, an urban myth that existed in the most rural of settings in the middle of nowhere on a tiny one lane bridge. People were told to go out at night, turn off the car, and call out, "Sally, Sally, come out to play!" Circling the car three times became part of the ritual. She would then appear, a haunting spectre, slowly walking up from a muddy grave, closer and closer. Any attempt to escape would be futile. The car will not start until she reaches the roadway.

Today the place still has a lonely feel to it. The road is out on the middle of nowhere, outside of Lincolnton, past a lazy bend that would take a car into a rather dramatic narrow spot on the short one lane bridge. Visitors beware, this is not an urban legend to test. There probably is less to fear from poor Sally than the road itself. There is no place to pull over. While the road may be infrequently traveled, it would be a grave mistake, no pun intended, to stop on the bridge and turn the headlights off.

Caroleen Bridge

Caroleen 35.28197° -81.80124°

Caroleen may be little more than yet another old mill town, a spot on a map that has its best days behind it. The remains of the mill and its requisite dam are about all that is left of the heyday of the community. The ghosts are quiet if they are still in the town. At least they are also polite, as has been discovered by the occasional passerby in a car.

In 1943, two spinster sisters were traveling back from South Carolina to their home in Caroleen. It was late, and an evening thunderstorm had rolled in, socking down the atmosphere so it was thick, dark, and rainy. It was just about the worst weather two little old ladies could be driving in. They thought they were fortunate enough to be close to home as they approached the Second Broad River Bridge just before their hometown. Just then, a truck approached them as they came up to the narrow bridge. With the headlights dazzling the ladies, and the dizzying effect of the large vehicle racing up seemingly to run them over, and the slick dark rainy road, the women lost control of the car. It crashed through the railing of the bridge, plunging to the bottom of the river, killing the two ladies.

Now, especially at night, and especially on rainy nights, two little old ladies can be seen just before the Caroleen Bridge. Kindhearted strangers have been known to pick up the two, who then tell the driver where they live, and politely thank the driver for stopping. It is only when they cross the bridge that something strange happens. The two polite little old ladies vanish from the back seat. The only things that are left of their visit are two damp spots, wet from the rainsoaked clothes the women wore.

They still are just trying to get home.

Mountains

Lake Lure Inn & Spa

Lake Lure   35.43066° -82.23047°

When the sun glistens off the ripples of dreamy Lake Lure during the day, or when all the boats go in and the stars come out to a quiet sleepy night on the alluring waters, the thoughts of ghosts may be far off the minds of vacationers looking to relax in the peaceful mountain village. What spirits are along the waters seem as restful as the living guests. A night in the 1927 Lake Lure Inn & Spa will whisk away guests to a bygone time, with its period decorated lobby, accented with statues and old kalliope music boxes. One would almost expect to see ghosts in tuxes and tails and long sparkling evening gowns wander through the lounge, or happy go lucky couples in long swim costumes, splashing in the tiled pool, blue water mixing with their own transparency.

The inn may either have ghosts, or just a paranormal presence. Suspected otherworldly guests include the creator and owner of the lake and inn, Lucius Morse. His visage has been seen late at night in the dining room. Employees have compared the ghost with a portrait hanging in the hotel and find them eerily similar. He may even walk the stairs of the inn late at night.

The spa is located in the downstairs of the inn. Workers have heard voices coming from the spa late at night, calling the employees by name. Several paranormal investigators have visited the spa at night, getting rather interesting EVP recordings. Whoever remains down there seems to call out to the employees, but not like others being down there in the evening.

Room 215 of the old inn is said to be haunted by a woman who was murdered in the room back in the 1930s. A lady was staying at the inn with her man, and she spent some time flirting with someone else in the lounge, possibly a highway patrolman visiting from the nearby retreat for the officers. In a jealous fit, her husband killed her in the room. In recent years, a woman in a long dress has been seen in the room and sometimes in others. She has been known to tuck people into their beds, ensuring a not so restful sleep for the unwitting guest. She has also been seen floating through the second floor hallway.

TVs sometimes turn on in the old inn, and objects have moved or glasses have broken. There is no specific presence that has been attributed to these actions. Considering the age of the old inn, there could be multiple spirits there, or just the remnants of some unknown presence, a quiet residual haunting.

The 1927 Lake Lure Inn & Spa has embraced the haunted aspect of their hotel. During the winter, while most of the town rests after a long summer and fall, the inn opens its doors to investigators from across the state and beyond for a paranormal conference. It allows for talks and meetings of ghost hunters, but also chances to explore the hotel, free of the summertime guests to get in the way.

But summer is the best time to explore the inn. Is it better for ghosts? No, probably not. Visitors may never see a single ethereal cloud or spooky ghost. But the air is warm, the water is cool, and the view is wonderful. A ghost free vacation is sometimes the most alluring escape.

Lodge on Lake Lure

Lake Lure   35.42534° -82.19307°

If the old Inn & Spa in Lake Lure isn't your cup of tea, there's an even fancier place along Lake Lure to stay. The Lodge on Lake Lure is a little more hidden, over on an eastern side of the lake. It feels more modern, having only opened in 1990. The rooms have a clean feel to them, with a mix of classically chic appointments combined with modern function. The bathrooms offer either a clawfoot tub or a glassed in shower, for example.

A couple of other rooms offer the ghost of highway patrolman George Penn.

The Lodge is modern looking now, but it was built in 1938 as a retreat for road weary highway patrolmen. Families could drive in or land a seaplane in the glassy lake, where they would rest in the peaceful isolation. It was named after George C. Penn, who was the first highway patrolman killed in the line of duty in North Carolina when he was gunned down by two criminals who had stolen a truck. Soon after his death, the land was purchased to build the retreat, and was named after the fallen hero.

It was turned into the lodge it is today, and now anyone can stay there. The high end hotel is nice and fancy, with views of the lake and grounds. Not only is a sit down breakfast served, they also do a wine and cheese evening service, and put out cookies and tea for anyone wanting a late night snack.

Which means that someone running through the empty great room late at night might find it not so empty. The ghost of George Penn might just be there. He also seems to like rooms 4 and 2. He has been seen to walk through 4 by guests. In Room 2, perhaps an apt number, he isn't seen, but he does play the trick of stealing the toilet paper from the bathroom. Guests to the room have been known to have to go to the lodge office to get a roll, even when they just stocked it.

One of the most famous tales of the haunting of George Penn is when a girl heard the legend of his ghost while staying there. Having seen nothing of Penn's ghostly visage during her stay, one evening in the great room she stated, "I wish that old ghost would do something!"

Immediately, a glass, sitting on the piano nearby, flung itself off and flew across the room, crashing to the floor and shattering. No one stood anywhere near the piano at the time. Careful what you wish for.

The Lodge on Lake Lure is a rather fancy place to stay just to see a ghost. The high end rooms can command high end prices. Guests that stay there do so to enjoy just such accommodations. The lake beckons with a boat dock, canoes, swimming, and sunning on the rooftop deck. Breakfast is included in the price, with a fine dining feel along with a great view. Evenings in the great hall with the large fireplace and a glass of wine are good for socializing with the other guests or winding down from a hot day on the lake. Afterward, when the other guests have gone to bed, the lodge is quiet, the dark night creeps in through the windows. A night owl guest wanders into the main room to steal a cookie or get a bucket of ice for nightcaps in the room. It is then that the wonderfully spooky and eerie feeling comes upon you. You are alone, but not alone.

Somewhere, George Penn watches and chuckles as you go by, looking over your shoulder, whistling in the lodge late at night.

Chimney Rock State Park

Chimney Rock   35.43213° -82.24953°

To start off, Chimney Rock is more of a legend than an actual haunt. Wait, Chimney Rock is real, the stories of it being haunted are more legends than hauntings.

Chimney Rock got its start the same way Lake Lure did, as a money making business for Lucius Morse and his family. He bought up the land of Chimney Rock to create a tourist location for people to climb up and look over the Hickory Nut Gorge and the twisting French Broad River. The land, including the namesake rock, were bought in 1902 and opened to tourists to climb and enjoy the view. In 1949, an elevator was added after having 258 feet of granite blasted out of the mountain. In 2006, the land was bought and ownership was transferred to North Carolina to become a state park.

But the legends of Chimney Rock predate all this by decades, or even a century. Before tourism, before the regular visits to the area, when the land was still rugged and empty, with fewer visitors from not so nearby Asheville, Black Mountain, or Hendersonville, there were a couple of strange sightings around the rock. On July 11, 1806, a little girl named Elizabeth Reaves, who lived nearby, saw a man on Chimney Rock. At the time, no one did mountain climbing, especially on the sheer rocky chimney out of the mountain. A man on top would be strange indeed. She told her brother, who pooh-poohed the idea as the imagination of a young child. That is, until he, too, saw not only one man, but hundreds or even thousands of people all around the rock, flying in a white angelic vortex around the giant granite monolith. All in all, six people witnessed the flock of white clad flyers. The angelic beings perched on Chimney Rock, then ascended through the clouds.

The account is so well known because it was later printed in a newspaper article, citing the family by name.

This wasn't the only heavenly flight seen around Chimney Rock, though. A few years later, witnesses would tell of seeing winged cavalry horses with riders upon them flying through the sky over the rock and lake. After several days, the riders formed into two groups and clashed in the sky, fighting an aerial battle with clashing swords. After only a few minutes, one side came out victorious, pushing the vanquished to the horizon, then riding on into the approaching darkness.

Many witnesses claimed it was some form of heavenly re-enactment of a Revolutionary War battle. Others saw it as a more spiritual battle, a dramatic portrayal of a final battle for the earth and its inhabitants.

To this day, the stories seem to be more fable or mystery than anything else. They have little value in more modern presumptions of ghostly tales. But the legends are important, as they may have some link to earlier stories, which also may have grains of truth within the legends. Lake Lure and the Hickory Nut Gorge area are rife with legends of natives to the area. With the narrow gap of the French Broad River to pass through, the land was easily defended by any native to the land. In early times there may have been a group of natives known mostly as the Little People, in Cherokee the *Yunwi Tsundsdi*. They were rumored to be similar to European legends of fairies or dwarves, creatures who lived in harmony with nature, and due to their small stature, literally closer to the earth. They blocked the way for Cherokee to pass east, being mysterious and magical to other tribes. Legend tells that a shaman for the Cherokee finally turned himself into a whirlwind to terrify the Little People, sending them in all directions, and scattering boulders all around the land as a result.

Another legend that lingers there and other places is the tale of the Moon Eyed People. This tribe of small, pale skinned people lived in the mountains of the area, and were known for their sensitivity to light. They could see better under the light of a moon than with the brightness of the sun. The mysterious Moon Eyed People were taboo to the other natives, and may have been feared for their differences by the Cherokee or other tribes. There are many anecdotal tales of pale skinned natives, sometimes called "Welsh Indians" due to a legend that had Welsh colonists coming over to the New World in the 1100s, long before Columbus made his journeys. The Moon Eyed People may also be groups of aboriginals that had albinism, turning their skin pale white and affecting their eyes to create photosensitivity to bright sunlight. The unique and rare affectation would have created both a shunning effect by the tribe, in order to not continue the genetic predisposition, but also the fear taboo of something different that the tribe as a whole did not understand.

Legends and myths continue through time, often changing only when the explanation no longer makes sense. The need for the myth, the tales, goes on. In order to replace the little people, the fairies, the Moon Eyed nighttime dwellers, new stories are developed and told, adding and sometimes supplanting the old myths.

Of course, these things spotted in the sky over Chimney Rock could be different stories entirely. A flock of birds, a rolling set of thunderstorms, the rumbling of nearby Rumbling Bald, where rocks fall inside the mountain and shake the towns, who knows what caused the stories? It helps keep the tales alive.

So keep watching the skies!

Green Park Inn

Blowing Rock   36.11846° -81.6605°

Hotels are great places to be haunted. It could be the tranquility of the offseason, with rooms so empty and halls so quiet that the only guests there would be the eternal ones. Perhaps the small rooms and long, narrow hallways with the endless repeating patterns of carpet close in on visitors, creating a claustrophobia inducing feeling of someone close at hand, yet never seen. Older hotels, with their prominent guests, long and strange history, especially if that history includes a death, are particularly notable for their haunts.

Opened in 1891, the Green Park Inn, located in Blowing Rock, checks all these boxes. It has ghosts and legends throughout the hotel. Room 318 holds the most famous ghost, that of Laura Green. A daughter of one of the founders of the original hotel, she and her fiancé would often meet in this room. After being left at the altar, Laura hanged herself in 318. She is said to haunt the room, but other stories say it is her lover that comes back, looking for her to make things right. The smell of smoke from his pipe pervades the air of the room.

Other rooms in the hotel have a more malevolent feel to some ghost hunters. Unable to determine any specific presence, the rooms still give off an evil vibe.

Around Room 210 is another of the more famous haunts of the hotel. People have reported hearing the footsteps and playing of children in the area. The soft padding of feet, and the giggling of kids has been heard late at night by guests. There is no real history for children to be there haunting the room or the hotel, but some have purported that there are the ghosts of two children, aged 10 and 11, that still play in the hall.

Room 131 plays host to a man who killed himself while staying at the inn. The old library has had reports of a shadowy figure that lurks in the darkened corners. The staff has reported organ and piano music coming from nowhere, heard in certain rooms and in the ballroom. There may even be presences left over from before the hotel was built, as it was partially constructed on an old Civil War fort in the area.

The Green Park Inn fell on hard times and closed for a while, only to reopen with new owners, who have slowly been fixing up all the rooms. The hotel embraces its haunted past, even including a ghost journal for guests to describe any experiences they have. In the past it encouraged ghost hunters to come to visit, and held paranormal conferences on the site. Curiously, the hotel also sits right upon the eastern Continental Divide. The hotel bar, The Divide is known for being on the exact boundary, thus the name. There is no information on what the ghosts like to drink.

Why We Look

A Spooky Side Trip

Michael La Chiana is a co-founder of The Heritage Hunters Society, a North Carolina based paranormal investigation group. Michael is one of, if not the, most respected ghost hunters in the state. He is also a very diligent investigator, with tons of experience. Michael is good at driving his examinations of potential haunts, with both an open and willing mind, coupled with a very rigorous demand for truth. Here he gives a little history on the drive of a good paranormal investigator.

Having always had a fascination with supernatural and ghostly tales I had heard as a child, I wanted to learn more about the unseen world around us. I always enjoyed watching the early 1970's TV shows such as In Search Of, Dark Shadows, The Night Stalker, The Ghost and Mrs. Muir and many more. So it was no surprise that I eventually became involved in the Paranormal Research and Investigation field.

While living in North Carolina for the last 25 years, I became very interested in studying the state's rich and haunted history. I always questioned how real paranormal activity could connect with historical locations I had been visiting through the years.

In 1992, I established The Heritage Hunters Society with my long time friend John Brennan, to help find possible answers to the age old question "Do Ghosts Really Exist?" And the answer, in my opinion is "Yes." They most certainly do...

Albert Einstein proved that all the energy of the universe is constant and can never be created or destroyed, it must then be transformed into another form of energy. I feel we are all energy based and when our physical body fades, we continue on in many different forms. I have felt static energies and temperature changes at many haunted locations. I have witnessed battery drainage and equipment malfunctions too many times as activity spikes. (*It is believed that ghosts, in their attempt to manifest themselves, drain energy from electrical devices and from the air. –J.S.*)

Using top notch equipment on locations such as Digital Recorders/Cameras, Infrared, Thermal, Full Spectrum video cams is important. Also having odd personal experiences during investigations is very important as well. Multiple factors help determine what is real data and what is not.

Capturing good photos, videos and audio clips which I then share with other close friends and team members during case review is crucial. We all try to debunk each questionable clip and vote on them to see what the group feels is solid or not.

Do I ever use Ghost Boxes, The Ovilus or any Ghost Apps? Never. I feel they just don't give enough good tangible evidence to support real paranormal activity.

99% of the time most claims are not paranormal at all, but it's that 1% of the time that is really worth researching and exploring the unknown.

Michael La Chiana
Founder/Director
The Heritage Hunters Society
www.theheritagehunterssociety.com

Phantom Hiker

Grandfather Mountain   36.09593° -81.83215°

As part of the ancient mountains of the Appalachians, an old man has slumbered peacefully, his beard growing brown and then white with the change of seasons. Near the town of Linville is the resting place of Grandfather Mountain. It was so named because the ridge of the mountain peaks resembles the profile of an old man with a beard, his head stretched back in permanent restful recline. During the winter snowfalls, his beard turns white as the crests are covered in a thick blanket of winter whiteness.

Grandfather Mountain has always been there, though it was originally called *Tanawha* by the Cherokee. It was later given the name Grandfather by pioneers who moved into the region later on. Bought by Donald MacRae in the late 1800s, the mountain's current popularity as a tourist stop was developed by MacRae's great grandson, Hugh Morton. Morton upgraded the road to the top viewing point and put in a swinging bridge to connect two high peaks, for visitors to more easily access the vistas. From there, people can see out across a wide expanse of mountains and valley land, a territory so diverse that it has sixteen different ecosystems as the mountain rises up from the valley and rivers and streams.

Visitors often make it to the viewpoint, the upper parking lot of Grandfather Mountain. When they take in that open tree lined land beneath them, they may not realize that crisscrossing the mountain is a series of hiking trails, diverse in environment and in difficulty. And, unless they get out on one of those trails, they may never know that the old Grandfather is home to another old man on the mountain. He's the Phantom Hiker.

There is little known about the phantom hiker, as far as legend or history goes. His appearance is always the same, though he seems to appear on different trails all over Grandfather Mountain. He is seen, usually passing hikers in the opposite direction, with a more rugged mid century outfit on, none of the modern light gear for him. He carries his pack, a rugged and beat up bag, made of leather and canvas. His face is set in concentration, as far as others can tell. He wears a long beard, and has never been seen to smile, speak, nod, or make any eye contact with others.

Legends mostly tell of seeing the old man, but no one knows who he was. He will pass by, not acknowledging the other hikers. When they turn to see where he is going, he vanishes, even in open ground where there is no cover to hide or tree line into which he would disappear. Some think he may be the ghost of a naturalist who lost his life out on the trails in a fall off a cliff. Others suppose that he merely is the spirit of a hiker from long ago. He enjoyed the peace of Grandfather Mountain so much that he remained after death to continue to walk the trails.

The Phantom Hiker has been spotted fairly often by other hikers on the trails. No one seems to agree on where he may show. The most likely trail, and one that several hikers have seen the man, is along the Profile Trail, which leads up from the valley road across the face of Grandfather, to the parking lot. The trail base starts off of Highway 105 at a parking lot at 36.12196° -81.82957°, which is marked with a sign for parking for the Profile Trail.

Be forewarned, hiking in general can be strenuous. Some paths are easy walks, while others require hand over hand passage, and footing can be tricky, to say the least. The Profile Trail, in its entirety, is long, with difficult sections to climb. Even experienced hikers will arrange to have a car at the top of the mountain, rather than hiking down in the dark. Food, water, good gear, good shoes, good health, all are needed to attempt any hike like this. People who haven't done something like this before should start slow, and go with guides and more experienced hikers.

That said, Grandfather Mountain has more to offer than just a ghost and a view. There are many hidden caves and crevices throughout the land there. The legends of the land are far older than the hiker, or the name Grandfather Mountain. It was believed that there were entrances to the underworld hidden throughout the mountain. They were marked by bubbling springs and guarded by fierce and hidden tribes of little people, similar to the tales told of the tribes around Lake Lure.

Grandfather Mountain holds a lot of secrets in its cool air. A summer visit would be just the ticket to cool off after the rest of the state heats up. Just watch your step, and say hi to that old man passing you. He may not answer, but it's still polite.

Warren Wilson College

Swannanoa   35.61276° -82.4401°

W arren Wilson College benefits from its humble roots as an educational institution that was founded in the mountains of North Carolina. Originally created by the Presbyterian Church in 1894 as a school for boys to get a high school education and training for agricultural and farm work, Warren Wilson College was first known as the Asheville Farm School. It would join with the Donald-Bell School to later become a secondary school, and by 1967 it was a four year college. Warren Wilson College is known for a unique educational and work ethic, where part of the college experience is being employed at the school in a regular job as well as participating in community involvement.

Incoming students may not know it upon entering both the campus and their time in college, but they will be brushing up with their skills on interacting with spirits from another time. Warren Wilson College is loaded with ghosts.

Tales of the supernatural abound in the college. It is hard to determine which have some tie to history, which are the fruits of a college student's burgeoning imagination, and which are hokum. There just seems to be a lot of them.

The Kittredge Community Arts Center is haunted, possibly by its namesake, Helen Kittredge, a donor and supporter of the college. The ghost will move items, set pieces, props, from place to place, and also reposition lights. While some suppose it is Helen Kittredge herself that does this, it could be equally likely that it is either some unnamed theater spirit, or even a misguided prop master moving things.

The Admissions building has been haunted since before the founding of the school, based on the legend that is attached to it. Staff at the Norland building will attest to seeing a ghostly apparition walk through the halls. A shadow of a man will pass by open doors, but when someone looks out, there is no one to be found. The ghost is said to be the remnant of a wounded soldier, brought back from Gettysburg by a compassionate young woman. Fearing her father's scorn, with the mountain area of North Carolina being strongly pro Union and anti slavery, she kept the man in the attic, tending to his wounds. While she cared for him, she began to care for him in a different way. The girl fell in love with her wounded soldier. Sadly, her father found out. Rather than throwing the man out, he did the more savage step of boarding him up inside the attic, so that the wounded man would suffer and die in the dusty upstairs.

The tale is most likely just a tale, untrue and only meant to create a bloodcurdling story for the incoming freshmen. The ghost may actually be there.

One curious tale doesn't entirely include a haunting. It may be a past history returning to the land. One of the residence halls, Sunderland, was once a place for slaughtering cows. Remember, Warren Wilson College was once a farm school, where students learned a very hands on practice of running a farm. Students have told of hearing the cows still in the basement, and of the stench of blood from the slaughterhouse that their home once was.

Sadly, the final tale has the creepiest source yet, but it no longer is in the original place. The portrait of Sarah Wilson that hung in the dining hall was seen to be possessed, for lack of a better term. Her eyes had creeped out enough people that one couple, during their wedding reception, covered the portrait with a cloth so as not to have Sarah staring over them. Bad luck would follow the party soon after, as the power went out inexplicably to the building, and only returned when the guests had left.

The campus seems to be loaded with these tales, more so than most other universities. There are haunted dorms, ghostly children, spooky security guards, and even a strange vortex hidden in the hills. The odd thing is, there really is little to back up the claims. Not many people talk about them, and there is nothing much to lend credence to the veracity of the stories. In addition, while visiting the campus would be worthwhile as it is a beautiful place, most of the haunted areas would be off limits to visitors who aren't staff or students. Which would make the people looking for the ghosts seem even creepier than the ghosts.

The Pink Lady of the Grove Park Inn

Asheville 35.62072° -82.54209°

There may be hotels with more ghosts in them than the Grove Park Inn, but there probably isn't a more famous haunted hotel anywhere in the state. The ornate hotel has been the mainstay for the famous since it was built in 1913, adding to the city's claim for fancy abodes with Biltmore being built a few decades earlier.

Guests enjoy the high end accommodations of mountain view rooms, tennis and golf on site, and a spa with an underground grotto pool. The stay is worth the high cost. The hotel has a history of fancy guests to match its fancy amenities, including ten presidents, Harry Houdini, and F. Scott Fitzgerald, and it even includes a ghost. The ghost may once have been a guest, but now is something more like staff.

The Pink Lady of the Grove Park Inn is one of North Carolina's most famous ghosts. She is the spirit of a young woman who was staying in room 545. Legends tell different stories of her demise. Most seem to think she was meeting her lover in a regularly scheduled rendezvous at their usual room. Upon arriving, the man broke off the relationship suddenly and in a fit of grief, the woman, dressed in her fancy pink dress, flung herself over the balcony to her death. A lesser discussed option was that the woman was actually a girl who worked for a man of stature in the town. The two would meet for secret trysts at the hotel. When the servant girl revealed that she was pregnant, the man flung her from the balcony in order to be rid of two problems for him at once. Still other tales simplify the ghost story by having a guest in a pink dress simply slip and fall, sending her tumbling to her demise.

However she met her end, it really wasn't the end for the Pink Lady. She has shown up often at the hotel. Sometime she is near formless, a gauzy ether of pink, a ghostly chiffon, that floats through the halls. Other times she is completely solid. Guests have held conversations with the oddly well dressed woman without knowing she was of another world.

The Pink Lady seems to be happy in her haunted hotel. And why shouldn't she, at the Grove Park? She has been known to play with children, and legends specifically tell of her comforting sick children stuck in bed at the hotel. She will occasionally play pranks on guests to her room, moving things from their suitcases, placing items around the room. She has been known to let her presence be felt by sitting on the edge of the bed at night, sometimes frightening the guests awake, and having them, sleepy eyed and weary, demand for accommodations fit for humans only. Living humans, that is.

Seeing the Pink Lady may be difficult. Well, she has turned up often in the hotel. People have been taking pictures, opening doors for her, watching her walk down the hall, until she vanishes. So she's being seen. The difficulty may just be in getting a room. The place is not cheap. On the plus side, guests will be really relaxed when she pops into their room. People have even started requesting Room 545, which may make it harder to get. The hotel, which in the past has downplayed the ghost, has recently opened up about their belief in the haunting, realizing it helps bring more lodgers. The Pink Lady isn't currently on the paid staff. She does get a free room, though.

Helen's Bridge

Asheville   35.59547° -82.53813°

A bridge is supposed to be a connection between two points. What was once a chasm is joined by a span, bringing two places together. Bridges are supposed to be a middle. Not an end. The bridge up on Beaucatcher Mountain in Asheville has a famous legend that has a very direct ending, with the loss of a woman's life right on the bridge.

Helen's Bridge is also known as the Zealandia Bridge, named after the estate at the top of the mountain which was home to John Evans Brown, an American who had traveled to Australia to make his fortune, only to return to Asheville when he inherited a large tract of forest in Buncombe and neighboring counties. After his death it was sold to Philip Henry, an Australian with a penchant for horse riding. He built a massive stable onto the estate, and added a bridge in 1909 to connect the neighboring peak to his land in order both to ride and for carriages to more easily cross.

The ghost of Helen appears sometime after this construction. Helen lived nearby, and was a resident or worker at the estate. Helen was the mother of a young daughter, and sadly the daughter died in a tragic fire on the estate. Helen, distraught with grief, could no longer go on with her life without her daughter. She tied some rope around her neck and flung herself off the tall bridge.

As is the case in tragic deaths, Helen's spirit could not leave the world so easily. For years people have seen the ghost of Helen, wandering the bridge, the road beneath, and the nearby woods. The gauzy specter appears in the evening, on those typically cool and misty nights in Asheville, calling and bemoaning the loss of her child.

She will ask the unsuspecting driver if they have seen her child, not knowing that she will never see the girl again.

The legend gained traction as people reported seeing the ghost, and additions have been made to the tale over time. Some suspect Helen was more than just a young woman on the mountain. Tales add on the idea that she may have been the mistress of Philip Henry, and killed herself when she discovered she was pregnant. Other tales include the more modern urban myth of calling out to her, saying "Come forth Helen," and she will appear. The road under the bridge has been the sight of the occasional stalled car. When passing under at night, the car engine will stall, headlights go out, and the night gets unnaturally eerie. The car will not start until it has coasted all the way to the end of the road. Helen is hoping someone will get out and help her look for her long lost daughter.

Helen's Bridge is located on College Street, off of Vance Gap Road, up on Beaucatcher Mountain. The location is well known to locals, and was even made famous in Thomas Wolfe's novel, *Look Homeward, Angel*. People go there to photograph it often. Zealandia Estate is still there, though it is on private property. It does hold a certain mystique, but it is not so important to see that going there uninvited is a good idea. The best views of the bridge are from underneath. Just watch out for the lady in the long flowing dress.

WhiteGate Inn

Asheville   35.60307° -82.55013°

The 1889 WhiteGate Inn and Cottage is as cozy a bed & breakfast as one would think with a name like that. It has two rooms, eight suites, and a cottage all available to the traveler looking for a quiet, homey alternative to the same old hotel room. Period furniture and appropriately chichi décor for a house of this style make it a great place to relax after walking the hip pathways of Asheville. The rooms are all named after famous authors. One room even has a pleasant ghost to help with the service.

Marion (or sometimes Merriam) Bridgette was an owner of the house back in 1928. She was a nurse in Asheville, and bought the house as her home. Her bedroom is now the Robert Frost Room. She will open and close drawers, doors, or turn lights on and off. She seems to be content with someone staying in her room. About the only strange thing that happens is that items can move inexplicably from one room to another.

Another spirit may also reside in the house, but, fortunately, it seems to stay in the basement. Only reported as a malevolent feeling, a wall of discomfort of sorts, there seems to be some strange presence down below the house.

A third ghost is thought to be in the house, too, but so little is said or known about the female spirit, it could just be some residual effect of Marion in the rest of the house. She has even been reported to sit in the Inn's gardens.

If anyone wants to experience Mrs. B, the best bet is to request her room, the Robert Frost Room. She may or may not show, but at least they will get a good night's stay and a tasty breakfast.

Chicken Alley

Asheville   35.59796° -82.55338°

Alone figure taps his cane as he walks the darkened streets of Asheville. Though the night is late and cool, the area he walks is lively with the drunken revelry that permeates the mountain town. Shadows darker than dark hide in every nook, with light only spilling out as a door opens for a moment. There are others on the street, all in town with trouble on their minds. The town is attractive to the many men who work in the nearby forests, loggers and lumberjacks with enough money to burn on liquor and easy women. If they see the man as he walks into the alleyway, they pay no heed. In a long black duster and wide brimmed black hat, he is easy to recognize as a regular, a local to the area. His wooden cane *tap tap taps* its way along the stone alley, with the occasional glint of silver from the handle, showing its owner is well off, successful. Ever present is his black bag, the signature tools of the trade for a doctor. It is late, and Dr. Jamie Smith heads toward Broadway Tavern.

He is not making a house call.

Dr. Smith, well to do, a doctor of means, means to have a good time. He is known to imbibe at night, and treat the same people he frequents during the day. Assuredly, much of his money comes from the treatment of diseases these loggers get at the hands of the prostitutes who reside in the area. He does nothing to hide who he is; his signature black hat and coat may hide his figure, but there is no mistake who wears this garb. When the man in black shows up, it is definitely Dr. Smith, and a rowdy time sure will follow, like death and taxes.

This night, hell would be inside the tavern, and death would follow.

When Dr. Smith entered into the Broadway Tavern, a bloody fight was already engaged. Not wanting fisticuffs to interfere with his drinking, Dr. Smith waded into the fight, his cane raised to deal damage. Any injuries he caused he could surely put right the next morning. Unfortunately for him, no one could fix the injury he received. At the hands of an unknown assailant, Dr. Smith was stabbed in the heart, killing him on the spot. Blood flowed freely where alcohol once poured, salting the tavern with his fatality.

The death would ultimately curse the tavern, as it would burn down to ash within a year.

The area would become known for both a more sanguine and a healthier pastime. Healthy for humans at least. The tiny alley would become a place where chickens were raised for slaughter, to be sold in a local market atmosphere. Where Dr. Smith fell, and the Broadway Tavern burned, Chicken Alley was born.

It wouldn't be long before residents would begin to hear a sound at night in the dark alley. Gone was the drunken revelry, but someone was still looking for a drink. *Tap tap tap* goes the cane. When someone looks out the window onto the dark street, they see him. Dark hat. Black coat. Doctor's bag. And the cane goes *tap tap tap...*

Chicken Alley has given up its past for a more colorful present. Now it is home to nice folks who stay in the apartments in the alley. They are used to visitors coming by to see the painted walls, the attractive artwork done by engaging street artists. Chief among them is Molly Must's tribute to the birds that gave their lives in naming Chicken Alley. An attractive hen gives visitors the eye as they wander into the old alley. She shows no fear of seeing old Dr. Smith as he walks the alley, late at night, in darkness. Still looking for a good time and   a   drink.

Riverside Cemetery

Asheville 35.60262° -82.56876°

Sure, a cemetery would obviously be haunted. Riverside Cemetery in Asheville has over 13,000 souls interred in the hallowed soil of this immense graveyard. Buried in Riverside are two famous authors of North Carolina, Thomas Wolfe and William Sydney Porter, of O. Henry fame. Two North Carolina governors, including Zebulon Vance, rest in Riverside, along with a larger number of congressmen and senators. There are even eighteen German sailors from World War I that are interred there. During the Great War, German prisoners were sent to Hot Springs for detention. When a typhoid epidemic rolled through, the sailors died, and were buried in Riverside, far from the cold rolling Atlantic Ocean. They nestle in the ground with soldiers from other wars, including a large number of Confederate troops, officers and enlisted, that found their final bed in Asheville.

With all those famous dead, you'd think that at least one would rise and haunt the place. No, all those souls rest peacefully in their graves. The grounds are haunted by a regiment of Confederate troops who fight a battle in the dark of night. Ghostly soldiers have been seen marching in formation, with the hollow sound of gunfire in the distance. The battle that takes place is short, and the soldiers vanish into the cool ether of Asheville's night, ready to take arms against the next Union raid into Asheville.

Riverside Cemetery is open to the public, but much of it is gated off so that cars cannot access the interior. Nearby UNC-Asheville is built upon most of the battlefield, and there are some earthworks left over from the time. Don't go into the graveyard at night. It may not have many ghosts, and those haunted soldiers' rifles may no longer be loaded, but any cemetery at night is dangerous, and usually off limits, with visits from the local Barney Fife to run trespassers in. Gotta nip that hauntin' in the bud.

Biltmore

Asheville   35.54063° -82.55262°

Scions of the great businessman William Henry Vanderbilt, and by that relationship, grandsons of Commodore Cornelius Vanderbilt, were the beneficiaries of the inheritance of possibly the richest will in the United States at the time. Cornelius Vanderbilt II and his brother William Kissam Vanderbilt would receive the bulk of the estate, while others would be properly provided for. The two eldest brothers would be put in positions of power for the Vanderbilt railroads, with trusted and experienced businessmen actually running the business while the brothers acted as figureheads.

The other children, unencumbered by business and the rigors of exceeding wealth, mere multimillionaires instead of hundred millionaires, lived their lives in various stages of hidden aplomb.

Cornelius II and William would each build massive mansions, including The Breakers and Marble House in Newport, Rhode Island. The youngest son, George Washington Vanderbilt II, was a favorite of his father. Quiet and introspective, he enjoyed reading, art, and philosophy. He happily allowed his older brothers to do the dirty work of the family business while he followed his own pursuits.

So it was that he traveled to Asheville with his mother, only to fall in love with the natural beauty and climate of the place. While his family built opulent mansions up north, he merely stated that he would build a "little mountain escape." The mountain chalet that the youngest son, the quiet philosopher, built took 1,000 workers over seven years to complete. When the bigwig brothers statesmen of the family came to quiet Asheville to see what their little brother had done, they were profoundly surprised to see he had built the largest house of anyone in the family, and would ultimately be the largest private house in the United States.

George Vanderbilt loved his home, with all the art that he collected over the years, all the furniture, all the guests and parties. But he also loved the land it sat upon. He created a large private forest along with formal gardens for the land around the estate. He wanted the land and home to be self sustaining. Ultimately, not only was there a winery and a dairy on the land, but an entire village was founded on the land with rental homes, a doctor, church, and school. Vanderbilt essentially created his own little European village.

George still had to follow the protocols of the wealthy of the time, entertaining guests with the necessary gild on every party that he threw. His parties were probably not first on his mind, though. Free not to worry about business, and with his home complete, George spent as much time as he wanted in his library. Only when his wife Edith would come call for him would he remove himself from the library and spend time with his guests.

George would pass on from complications from an appendectomy in Washington, D.C. in 1914. Even though he died in the nation's capital, his ghost seems to reside back in Asheville. More specifically, in the library of his Biltmore home. George has been seen as a dark figure, sometimes in a striped suit, a style of his time, in the library. He may have even been appearing soon after his death. Employees of the time reported that Edith would often go into the library and talk to George, a reminiscence to her lost love. What they noticed after a while is that, instead of shaking off her melancholy like they expected, she actually increased her discussions with her late husband. Then, inexplicably, the workers started hearing George's voice.

When Edith died, it didn't stop her from showing up to get George out of the library. Now people sometimes report seeing George in the library, and sometimes they hear a woman's voice calling, "George."

The other haunted area that generally is recognized is the underground indoor pool. The pool has long been drained of its water, with no need for it to be filled, as well as for the safety issue of visitors possibly falling in. Yet still people when nearby can hear the sounds of splashing and laughing, as if there still are guests in the Biltmore enjoying a party around the pool.

The three ghost stories have intertwined into one legend. George, introverted and happy in his library, enjoys a solitary cigar in his solitary chair. Edith, more social and more understanding of social responsibility, knows that George must make his appearance, the wealthy scion and star of Biltmore, so she goes to him and calls his name. George, following the obligations of wealth and American nobility, rises from his chair to attend to the fun loving party, centered around the pool.

One other ghost that makes the rounds at Biltmore is known as the Weeping Lady. She is seen, dressed in black, crying as though her heart is broken. Little, if anything, is known about the weeping lady. She has been seen gliding through the house, sometimes at the pool, sometimes in other places. The story of her is vague, as no one can determine if she died there, or lost someone else, which may be the cause for her grief.

The ghosts of Biltmore have been heard, more than seen, mostly by the staff, as they are around more often than a visitor that is shuffled quickly from one room to another. Guests are unlikely to see or hear anything in the busy home. Biltmore is open to visitors, with a fee. There are tours available to different parts of the estate, and once done, visitors are welcome to walk through some of the more public areas. The haunted spots, the library and the pool, are only available on tours, though.

Going to visit Biltmore isn't cheap. Just the regular pass to get on the grounds and walk around is a high priced ticket, with extra fees for going on tours. Even then, the ghosts may not show, probably won't show, in all honesty. Seeing Biltmore, well, it is a fascinating building, and the gardens are attractive. But it may be up to the individual to decide if the high cost is worth it. One piece of advice is to stay at the inn on the grounds. They often have tickets thrown in to the nightly stay, saving visitors a hefty chunk.

Inn on Main

Weaverville 35.69273°-82.55981°

One of the many great things about exploring the parts of North Carolina that don't adjoin an interstate is that there often is a cute little spot to stop and spend the night. Inns and B&Bs are the home away from home for the easygoing traveler, ready for a quiet night, some good stories with other guests, and a breakfast that consists of more than a pancake made by pressing a button. Sure, sometimes we just need sheets and a shower, but the road gets weary after a while. A little peace, a thicker wall, a softer bed... the darkness of a small town calls to us. The sidewalks roll up at night. Frogs croak and peep in the trees. Stars come out. There's no roar of cars and trucks speeding by into the midnight abyss of the never ending highway. We can go to bed early, snuggled into our sheets. If the ghosts are kind enough and keep their chain rattling down, we sleep.

The Inn on Main is a peacefully haunted little place, snuggled into its own set of sheets in Weaverville. While it isn't advertised as being haunted, there are a few tales of a ghost or poltergeist that may haunt the little inn. In addition to the usual doors opening and closing, there are other more specific events in the inn.

Before it was an inn, it was the home and clinic for a Dr. Zebulon Vance Robinson. Dr. Robinson would treat people in his home office, and often they would wait there, biding their time while the good doctor cared for someone else. Guests have reported seeing former patients in the rooms. One saw a young woman fixing her hair in the mirror. Another reported seeing a black man and a little girl, hazy and opaque as mist, when he woke up in his room. He asked the man what he was doing and the ghostly figure responded that he was waiting to see the doctor. Dr. Robinson was known to treat both the people in the town, as well as the more rural African-American community that lived nearby.

In addition to the patients still visiting the doctor's home, it may be that there is still some remnant of the doctor, or at least someone who cares about the house. The most famous legend of the inn is that when the owners, Dan and Nancy Ward, first celebrated New Years Eve there, they heard the sound of pictures crashing to the floor. Rushing in to see what had happened, they found the pictures, still intact, and hanging neatly from the walls. Dan believes that the ghost prefers the status quo, and as long as nothing big happens in the house, he won't hear from Dr. Robinson, or whoever it was, again.

The inn is a nice place, in a nice town. It would be a good stopping point on the way into the mountains, instead of the bright lights of Asheville. If there are any ghosts about, the Lee Room may be the preferable abode. This is where the young lady was seen. Dan reported hearing her call quietly to him, "yoo-hoo," from the stairs when he was on the second floor.

No word on what she likes for breakfast.

Hot Springs Hotel

Hot Springs 35.89622° -82.82612°

The art of the vacation has changed over the years, as can be seen by the different destinations in North Carolina that attracted families and travelers during the early days of destination travel. The Outer Banks that now floods with tourists during the summer was a popular winter respite for the wealthy from up north. The kids that once filled summer camps at lakes across the state now pack into their parents' cars and head out of state to Myrtle Beach. And the mountains that call to skiers today in the winter time with soft fluffy slopes were once a destination for the rich to spend the summer in opulent comfort, fully entertained at a mega resort.

Hot Springs, near the French Broad River by the Tennessee border, was one such destination. As early as 1832, a giant hotel set its footprint down by the river, taking advantage of the natural hot springs that drew in people wanting to take in the waters for health reasons, or merely to find a way to relax and relieve their stress. The Patton Hotel stood until 1884, when it burned down. It was quickly replaced by an even bigger resort, the Mountain Park Hotel, which had four stories of 200 rooms, all with electricity and steam heat from the local hot springs. Additionally, a bath house with deep marble tubs graced the land. Guests worthy of the experience would spend three weeks getting a soak and a massage every day. For a change of pace, they could play on the first golf course in North Carolina, built upon the same grounds. Swimming pools and theaters amused the wealthy guests, or they would find their way to the onsite bowling alley or billiard hall. Summer was surely the life of leisure for those fortunate enough to stay at the Mountain Park Hotel.

With the outbreak of World War I, tourism went into a decline. A flood also took its toll on the town. In 1920, the Mountain Park Hotel fell to an inferno. It would be understandable that an older hotel, made of wood, like the old Patton Hotel would go up in flames. Now a second one, too, one with more modern amenities and electric lights, had burned to the ground.

A third hotel, built as a sanitarium, but never used, fell into disrepair and also burned.

Was there a simple, earthly cause to the fires? Was there a curse? Or was it something else? The area of Hot Springs was for a long time an important place for the local Cherokee of the area, as well as for natives to the land that traveled through there. Nearby Paint Rock has ancient symbols that may have been traffic signs of a sort, marking a path through the mountains. The Cherokee presence on the area has lead to a ghostly legend. For the entirety of any hotel's existence in Hot Springs, a Cherokee man has been seen walking along the shore of the French Broad. He has appeared for almost two hundred years in the area, seen by guests of the different hotels since the 1800s.

Today, the old hotels are gone, burned to their foundations, with only an outline of stone and marble to show where the grand bathhouse was. In its place are much more sedate campsites, outdoor homes for campers who like being a little closer to nature. On the other side of the street, where the old hotel once stood, there are secluded hot tubs, filled from the hot springs and available for a soak for the hikers coming off the Appalachian Trail. Even people soaking in the tubs, isolated and private, with peaceful views of the river flowing past, have said to have seen the ghost of a Cherokee, keeping watch over the area once so important to his tribe.

There is an idea put forth that the positive energy and healing springs keep development in check around Hot Springs. Today it is a tourist destination with a popular artist collective, but it still hasn't gotten that big. Manmade growth seems to slow down there, keeping the place a sound throwback to simpler, easier times. Perhaps the ghost of the Cherokee is just keeping an eye on his stomping grounds, making sure nothing gets out of hand.

Cowee Tunnel

Dillsboro 35.376769° -83.267784°

Even though the abhorrent practice of slavery was abolished after the Civil War, wealthy and conniving industrialists, hungry for cheap labor, helped to create a de facto slave labor force for the back breaking construction of the railways into the mountains of North Carolina. African-American men were summarily arrested and convicted, usually on false or frivolous charges, and sent to prison, only to be placed on forced labor for building roads and train lines. Most of these people had never ventured far from the towns and cities where they were from, and had not experienced the wildness of mountain winters.

Thus was the beginning of a disaster and a shameful legend of history, and a very creepy ghost tale to boot.

In 1882, a group of prisoners would be sent to Dillsboro to work on the Western North Carolina Railroad, with the purpose to cut through a mountain to form the Cowee train tunnel. On December 30, the workers would receive no belated Christmas, no respite for the upcoming New Year. They would be awoken, shackled at the ankle one to another, and loaded upon a cheap boat that would be pulled across the cold Tuckasegee River. The prisoners, unused to such treatment and conditions, began to panic as the water sloshed in the boat. Thinking it was sinking, the men shook the boat, pleading to be pulled back, or just get to land. The swift and churning water did its worst, tipping the boat and its occupants over into the rushing frigid stream.

Most of the men had no ability to swim; it was never an option for them. Some were able to find a way to the far shore, only to realize they were attached by heavy chains at the ankles. One by one, the men were pulled inexorably into the water. The cold froze their bodies so they couldn't move. The chains pulled on them. Lungs gasped for air, and then gave way to the foregone end, as the men were swept underwater to a frozen and watery death.

Nineteen cold bodies were later recovered from the river. There were two warm bodies that made it out alive, though the story doesn't end well for one of them, either. Anderson Drake somehow slipped his bonds in the panic, and swam to shore. He saw a guard floundering in the icy water, and dove in to save the guard, Fleet Foster. Drake pulled the waterlogged man to shore, saving his life. It was said around camp that Drake was a hero, that he would surely go free after saving the man's life. Later, it was discovered that Foster's wallet was missing. A search of the camp turned up his wallet in Drake's possessions. Instead of being hailed a hero, he was flogged in camp, sentenced to thirty years hard labor, and put right back to work on the railroad.

The punishing work did its job. It got the railroad built, cheaply for the rail barons, and costly for the men who were forced to work and die on the road. It is thought that over 400 men died at the hands of the railroad. Who knows how many more were falsely imprisoned or just lost from society in that time.

With all the tragedy involved in the Cowee tunnel line, there is no wonder why the place is considered haunted and cursed. The dark tunnel bend has been the location of many train wrecks, derailments, and cave ins. The tunnel is said to cry with the tears of the men, all buried together in a mass unmarked grave above the tunnel. When passing through the middle of the tunnel, the ghostly sounds of picks chipping at the stone, and the wail of the men, forever suffering, has been heard.

The tunnel is only accessed by the Great Smoky Mountains Railroad, which takes people on train rides through the darkened tunnel. The only safe way to see the tunnel from the inside is by riding the rails. There is no foot access to the tunnel anyway, as it has old wooden trestle bridges on each side of the mountain, and the line is fenced off. A train ride in the fall, windows to the cars open with a cool breeze filling the air will be much more fun than stumping around the train tracks. Remember the history, but enjoy the ride.

Afterword

I have had the pleasure of talking, writing, and meeting with several paranormal investigators over the years of writing my books. Some are hobbyists, some are extremely serious. They do it part time, full time, as a job, for free to anyone who wants to know. None of them had proton packs or wear jumpsuits. At least, not when I met them; I judge not on fashion sense. I will say, they are all nice folks.

I wrote this under the duress of being, well, less of a believer, let's just say. A skeptic at the least. I understood the legendary stories well. I'd still love to believe that ghost pirates buried treasure at my beach, but I'm sure they didn't. The book was written to document the ghost stories and haunts of the state. I wanted to get all of them, or as many as I could. I wanted to avoid just another ghost book with the same stories everyone have already read. I hope I did that well for you, dear reader. But I also hope I did well for all of you who believe in ghosts. Yes, I'm a skeptic, but I understand that there are people who believe. I just want to say that I believe that *you* believe. I didn't get to see any ghosts this time. No voices, no mists, no scratches. I think I got beat up more writing my other books than this one, actually. I don't know why I don't find ghosts and some others do. They are just lucky that way.

I hope you enjoyed the book and the stories inside. I hope you get a chance to be outside and experience the stories yourself, as long as you stay safe, of course. Keep an eye out for those dark shadows. You never know what you might find.

Good ghost hunting!

-Joe Sledge   Sept 2017

The Rest of the Tale...

Most ghost stories and legends have both a tie to real historical events, and a decidedly imaginative bend to embellishment. In writing this book, I did the research on many places to find out how much of a story or legend was real. Sometimes history and the tale matched up very well, other times there was a bit of a stretch, though I could see where the story came from. Still others, well, they really had the feel of just something made up to scare someone. That doesn't mean that the ghost story isn't true; it just means that there is not any obvious evidence that lends credence to the story.

I was surprised to find several tales where the legend lined up very well with actual events. And sometimes the reports of ghosts are so clear, with no real reason to make things up, that there may be a ghost floating around out there. Somewhere.

If you want to know a little more about some of these stories, read on. You may be surprised. You may be disappointed.

You may not care and go on out to that creepy bridge anyway.

Currituck Light Keepers' House...

Every good legend benefits from retelling, and additions. Is this story true? Well... Sadie Johnson really did drown when she was a little girl. The only difference, and it's a major one, is that she died after she and the Johnsons had left the lighthouse. Sadie drowned in Virginia Beach, and was buried in the town of Waterlily. It is highly unlikely that her body would have been brought back to the lighthouse in the summer even if the Johnsons had still been there. There is no evidence of any other death in the quarters that match the other tales. The last keeper and his wife, Vernon and Bertha Gaskill, both lived well past the time of automation, with Bertha not passing until 1965, with no evidence of tuberculosis as the cause, and her passing was in Wanchese, on Roanoke Island, far from the Currituck shore. While there are tales of unease by visitors to the north room, none can be substantiated, and recent keepers have reported no paranormal experiences.

Curiously, there is a story that seems to add to the source of the legends, though the tale is sad but decidedly not paranormal. Loren Tillett with his wife Esmeralda served as the keeper of the light from 1921 until 1930, after having worked at the Potomoc River Lighthouse. He left that job after the loss of his daughter, Merle, who fell into the swift current of the river. Loren jumped in to save her, but the girl was too heavy and began to pull both under the water. He had to let his daughter go to drown in order to save his life, a horrific event for Loren. After moving to Currituck, he promised himself to care for his other children, and do his utmost to keep them safe. He would tell them to stay away from the dangerous waters of the sound and shore, as well as to avoid the ramshackle homes of fishermen and hunters who may snatch the children if they got too close. The kids tested their father, once, and he came to the beach, carrying a goose above his head, running around and honking like the bird, chasing the children playfully back to the safety of the house. By all reports, Loren was a loving and devoted father first, and everything, lighthouse keeper included, came a distant second. The loving story of loss turned into love may be a better fitting tale to the light, for a lighthouse is meant to be a protector.

The Whalehead Club...

That there are paranormal experiences and tales from the Whalehead Club there is no doubt. There are enough first hand reports of weird occurrences and strange feelings that there is little chance that the original firsthand stories are not made up. It's likely that many of these people who told the stories really did say that they experienced something. The difficult part is actually determining if there is anything to the stories. Since most hauntings occur due to death, especially tragic death, it is odd that a place so massively haunted has no documentation of any death there, except for the thousands of birds killed while hunting.

Furthermore, the legend that the Knights packed up and left in late 1933 may be erroneous. It is also documented that they attended every winter in Corolla until their deaths in 1936. So there are no real explanations as to why the psychic energy is so high and so many people are on edge when visiting the place.

The Ghost of the Black Pelican...

Essentially everything in the story is true, and has been backed up by more than one record of events. T.L. Daniels did die in the lifesaving station after pulling a gun on an unarmed Keeper Hobbs. However, the legend usually tells of his body being unceremoniously dumped at sea, and that the incident was somewhat covered up, with Hobbs being supported by his crew. In reality Daniels' remains were interred in the family cemetery. As for the events at the restaurant, they have been reported by numerous persons. Sliding plates and glasses happen often in places like this, and a dark old restaurant late at night can be somewhat off-putting, letting the mind play tricks. But most people would attest to what they saw or felt. It may be haunted. Just don't let that stop anyone from getting a bite to eat.

Nags Head Woods...

There still are remains of some old villages on the old sand road through Nags Head Woods. And people will, quietly, confess to seeing shadows in the trees, but there are no real specific ghost stories to attach to the area. Goat Man seems to have spawned from three separate events. The general Goat Man legend, where a scary monster inhabits a wood and torments innocent teenagers merely out late at night in the middle of nowhere to have illicit rendezvous, occurs in many states. It works well in Nags Head Woods. And there really was a person living in the little yellow house in Nags Head Woods. Calvert Duvall would live there, just to be alone and one with nature, not to torment anyone or anything. He wasn't even a hermit, just a guy who liked to go back in the woods to fish and explore. What tied all this together was probably a simple bit of vandalism. Either the Goat Man tale made the rounds orally, or someone went and spray painted "Goat Man Lives" on a road sign warning drivers that the old sand road was a twisty one. The legend was in print, so to speak, and would live on for decades.

Nags Head Woods is a nice place to visit in the day, but really just because of the danger of going out at night on a twisty road, where a car can get stuck, it's best to avoid the area, and its denizens, at night.

The Unpainted Aristocracy...

The ghosts of the Unpainted Aristocracy may be more likely from some person's creative imagination, rather than from any real legend. However, the ghost in the kitchen is a real tale, told by multiple people who stayed in the house. The home wants the location kept quiet, as the house is for private use only.

Other, less ghostly, but still odd tales pervade the Unpainted Aristocracy. Seven enslaved women, either sisters by blood or formed in chains, promised to stay together through their struggles until they could raise enough money to get home and free of servitude. They worked for an owner of one of the cottages at the time. Upon gaining enough money, the seven left, set out immediately for the freedom they sought. The next day a huge storm blew in, socking the Outer Banks with torrential winds. After the storm cleared, seven dunes had formed over the sound side of Nags Head. The Seven Sisters dunes stood until they were removed for a shopping mall.

Another tale centers around Dr. Pool, who would often treat the poor and destitute Bankers living on the sound near his beach home. One woman, elderly and not long for the world, received what care Dr. Pool could give, easing her pain as best he could. With no money, she gave him a portrait in oil of a woman that was hanging in her darkened house. The painting, she said, was taken from a ship that had been wrecked on the shore long before. She stated that the woman had been on the ship, and had died at the hands of the Breakers. The portrait turned out to be a painting of Theodosia Burr Allston, daughter of Aaron Burr, Vice President of the United States under Thomas Jefferson, and famously the man who shot and killed Alexander Hamilton in a duel. She had been returning to New York to see her father who had been on the run due to his many exploits. Her ship was lost at sea, and no one had known what had happened to her. The portrait hangs in the Lewis Walpole Library in Yale.

Ghost of the Roanoke Island Inn...

Manteo is blessed to be a quaint old town with a pretty waterfront, lots of shops and old buildings, and some beautiful homes and inns. The flip side to this is that with all the old buildings come a lot of strange stories and rumors. In addition to the Roanoke Island Inn ghost, there are supposedly haunts at the Tranquil House Inn, the White Doe Inn, as well as stories of strange shadowy ghosts called hoodoos that orbit the shore and fireplaces of houses in Mother Vineyard. In addition, tales of haunting by people who lived in the houses are told and repeated, even though the stories just aren't true. Legend often has an embellishment. Most of these stories are based on noises and just uncommon events. A glass breaking may be a bit of bad luck to a restaurant, but it is not proof of a ghost. Nor is a strange sound from a heater.

However, the ghost at the Roanoke Island Inn does have some credence. There is an actual form that has been seen. And there is a legitimate occurrence of loss in Roscoe Jones' story. Of all of the ghost stories in Manteo, this may be the most truthful tale.

The Gray Man of Hatteras...

If the Gray Man of Hatteras sounds familiar, that's because there is a very similar ghost story told down on Pawley's Island in South Carolina. The ghost even has the same name. The legend that sighting the ghost seems to come from there, actually, as a spirit of either a young man lost in a murky marsh, or it could be Percival Pawley or Plowden Weston, the namesake of the island and an early hotel owner, respectively. The ghost of Hatteras differs in that it seems to be a sailor in most of the lore. He has been given the moniker of "Gray," a not so subtle play on his appearance. Due to his appearing only before major hurricanes, and that Hatteras Island and Ocracoke are now evacuated well in advance of any approaching tropical storm to ease in traffic problems, it may be that the Gray Man has little chance to appear to anyone.

Cape Hatteras Lighthouse ...

The legend of the shadow people may just be a good ghost story to scare kids or tourists, but there are several graves under the sand, especially near the old site of the lighthouse. Many times bodies would wash up, unidentified, and with the water and sun doing damage to the dead flesh, the remains needed a quick burial. Who knows what rests, or doesn't rest, under the sand at Cape Hatteras.

Bob is a more curious legend in that little is ever said about the story. He is rarely sighted in most lore, and again, may just exist in legend. The name "Bob" could as easily come from him wearing a yellow jacket like a float bob for fishing instead there being any history to his story.

The cat? Who knows? Many people claim to have seen it. At least it is friendly, and probably doesn't shed.

The Flaming Ship of Ocracoke...

Cristoph von Graffnreid was a real Swiss baron, and the story has some serious parallels to real history. Von Graffnreid led a group of settlers from England to North Carolina, mostly in order for him to make money and pay off his debts in Switzerland. Along the way, the ship was attacked by French privateers who took everything the colonists brought with them for settling. This could be an origin for the story of the Flaming Ship. The colonists actually did make it to New Bern, albeit with nothing but the clothes on their back. Von Graffnreid would go back to England for more supplies and more colonists.

Oddly enough, von Graffnreid would meet a different threat in the New World, as he and explorer John Lawson had founded New Bern on an abandoned Tuscarora village. The Tuscarora captured the two, and planned to kill them, but they assumed von Graffnreid was the governor of North Carolina, due to his fancy clothes. They ultimately spared him in exchange for the "governor" promising not to retaliate for the capture. John Lawson was not so lucky.

Von Graffenreid would ultimately return to Bern and become a public official, living out his life in obscurity, though not without comfort.

The Flaming Ship legend may have other roots. Few people have ever even said they have seen the event, even over more than three hundred years. The paranormal event may have something tied in with a full moon. On a rare clear night, when the moon is full, and there is no haze or cloud over the horizon, an extraordinary series of events indeed, the moon can be seen to bubble up from the water. Its deep yellow light can look like a nighttime sunrise, and the light curves over the horizon, a near magical meteorological event, it may seem that there is a flaming ship rising up through the water, ready to sail its way into the shore. It could just be that whoever saw this may have run in terror, or they could have just run to the house to get the family and show it to them. By the time they get back, the ship is gone and the moon is high in the nighttime sky.

Or the flaming ship just sailed away.

Teach's Light...

The ghost tales of Ocracoke are a popular pastime on the island. The premonitions of locals as to their impending demise lead to predictions of the afterlife. Since the families are tight there, the surnames of Howard for many of the long time residents are not coincidences. They descend from a common ancestor, a crewmate of Blackbeard's that survived the attack and the hanging of his compatriots. Close attachment to ancestors, combined with old creaky houses, create a very good climate for ghost tales.

As far as Blackbeard, well, his ghost is said to not only haunt Ocracoke, but the town of Bath, and a promontory in Hampton Roads, Va. It is said that the pirate Teach was so evil that even the Devil wouldn't have him. Who knows where his restless spirit walks? Considering his bloodthirsty image, it might be best not to find out.

The Old Burying Ground...

The Old Burying Ground certainly is spooky and creepy, with the haphazard graves and low overhanging trees. But it probably isn't really haunted. Most likely a mixture of publicity for the story of the little girl, mixed with late afternoon shadows and people messing with the trinkets placed at her grave have given rise to the ghost story.

That doesn't mean that there aren't ghosts around. In a town that old, one of those places could quite possibly be haunted. Like maybe the Webb Library in nearby Morehead City...

Webb Library...

The usual suspects of a haunting, the creaking doors and footsteps, may be easy to explain away in an old building, but there is ample evidence gathered by investigators of ghostly voices and strange temperature changes to make this a very likely haunt. The book stacking is reminiscent of Ghostbusters, though, and very well may just be the act of pranksters and vandals. This probably is a good place for people to go looking for a spook.

The Cotton Exchange...

Some people have seen ghosts all over the place at the Cotton Exchange, some have been there 20 years without a creak or rattle to startle them. There are several photos of nebulous blobs that look like faces or shadows from tours of the buildings, which may or may not be the capture of a presence. The Cotton Exchange is a popular spot for ghost tours, so promotion may help inspire some tales. The sheer number of accounts means that people may see something, but what that might be is anyone's guess.

St. James Episcopal Church...

The legend is usually purported to be fact, in that there is documented evidence that Samuel Jocelyn was actually buried alive. Many legends use this to help fortify the tale. Considering the strength and believability of Samuel Jocelyn's tale, it probably happened, with some flash added to it for a good campfire tale feeling. Shadows in a graveyard are something else to see. There may be more than one floating around there.

Maco Light...

The Maco Light was absolutely real. Too many people saw it to discount its existence. From the average visitor to even noted North Carolina author Bland Simpson, lots of people saw the light. And famous writer of ghost stories and legends of the state, Nancy Roberts wrote about the tale. Included in her book was a photograph of the light by her husband Bruce.

What is not assured is the reason behind the light. The legend tells of conductor Joe Baldwin losing his head in a train accident. The reality is that no accident ever happened. There was a Charles Baldwin, who died in a train accident, but it wasn't actually a wreck. Charles simply forgot to put a lamp on a car that was to be coupled to a train, and the train impacted the car and him too hard, killing him. Charles was buried, head and all, in Wilmington. Curiously, his cemetery was later moved. Unfortunately for Charles, the grave markers were moved first, and when they came back for his grave, they forgot where it was. Charles Baldwin is buried somewhere in Wilmington in an unmarked grave.

Fort Fisher...

The ghostly tale of a figure on the mounds has a lot of backers. Many people have seen someone that looks ghostly there. The ghosts of the woods have been described as a memory of the land, an appearance of an event that happened at one time reappearing in the present. They could just as easily be shadows flickering from flashlights or car headlights.

One legend that has been debunked somewhat is the noise of war that is heard at night, especially on the beach side. Loud explosions or the firing of cannons can be heard by the shore. The noises have been documented, and do occur. They are likely sounds from the nearby nuclear power plant or the loading of shipping boxes at the nearby port.

The Brown Lady of Chowan University...

The story is old, even being passed into legend in the early 1900s with a legendary tale reported in the school newspaper in 1914. The legend must be very old indeed to have passed out of general knowledge and into lore even at that early time.

Students loved the story and the haunting. In the 1950s and 60s, upperclass students would take the young freshmen to meet Eolene. They would be blindfolded and escorted through the campus, where they would be told they were taken to her grave. Eolene would come out to meet the blindfolded students, where she would shake their hands. In reality, a student would stand in for the ghostly Eolene, her hand covered in ketchup to introduce the ectoplasmic spirit with the incoming students. They would walk over the "graves" of others, stepping into holes filled with egg shells and mud. After the fun house activities were over, the students would return to the campus halls for a party, and the freshmen would be welcomed as part of the school.

Somerset Place...

I have visited both Somerset Place and Pettigrew. While I didn't hear any screams or see the ghosts of any slaves, I got a great Polaroid of me standing in a tree, with a bright flash of a tree sprite in the photo. It was just such an odd thing. When I showed to others who had camped there, along with the local park service, they were nonplussed. "It's a tree sprite," they all said, like it happened all the time.

Lake Phelps is an interesting place. It is an ancient lake, about 8000 years old, and the water is surprisingly clear. Old dugout canoes have been found in the lake. Also, even though the water is somewhat acidic, bass are still able to thrive in the water even though they shouldn't be able to reproduce. Lake Phelps is almost perfectly round, and no one is entirely sure how the lake formed.

-J.S.

Screaming Bridge...

The legend obviously has changed with the times. Most likely the story has existed more to make up reasons for the strange sounds coming from the woods at night. Screams probably will be heard, but they are more likely to be the calls of an owl. Or someone hiding under the bridge if they know their friends are going later.

Hidden farther into the woods is the original bridge, where the legends say the earlier events happened. It's too far afield to wander around in the dark, or probably even in the light, to visit just for an urban legend.

Gimghoul Castle...

The story of Peter Dromgoole seems so farfetched that it can't be more than a legend. Oddly enough, most of it is actually true. Peter Pelham Dromgoole was a young man from a Virginia family, though his current lineage actually lived in Halifax County in NC for a time. Peter was sent in 1833 to attempt to earn entrance to UNC, but was not successful. He wrote his father that he was now working with a tutor to be able to attend in June. To further the family disappointment, his father, Edward Dromgoole II, received notice that his son was behaving poorly in the town, or at least in an unbecoming manner. Angered by his son's failure and his behavior, the two argued long distance by mail, culminating in Peter saying he would never grace his father's presence again. His roommate, John Buxton Williams, who would go on (in the legend only) to become the infamous competitor and ultimately killer, described Peter as a strange and moody kid. Peter would leave his roommate, and the town, leaving most of his belongings and all of his debt, to join the Army under an assumed name.

The duel and death also happened, though not to Peter, obviously. His uncle, a Virginia congressman, killed a man in a duel. The two stories combined to make a legend, and the big rock got thrown in for good measure.

Carolina Theater...

The Carolina Theater is ripe with weird stories, paranormal or otherwise. Most of what is in legend is completely true. There does seem to be a worker who fell from the building when it was being constructed. And there are many documents showing the fire and its sad cause. Melvalina, sometimes going by other names like Melvaleene or Melba, really did set fire to the theater and die in her undergarments. If the fire door to the stairs had not closed, the whole theater would have been lost.

The little boy story can be a little bit tougher to prove, but there's an odd twist to go along with it. Before the theater was built, there actually was nothing there. It was a public space, and it was used for a fairground or other outdoor public events. There was no home there immediately before construction. However, with the land so popular as an open spot, many kids played there, including one of Greensboro's favorite sons, William Sidney Porter, who went by the pen name O. Henry.

Lydia's Ghost...

The Lydia legend is a very famous tale from North Carolina. Surprisingly for many who have heard the story, the same one exists in many forms in other states. There is always a girl, stranded from a dance or date, and always picked up by a chivalrous man. He always takes her home, and the same woman answers the door. The mother never aged nor died. She always appeared when the door opened.

Most of this story can be chalked up to a campfire tale turned urban legend.

There have been reports by both ghost hunters and curious seekers of this famous legend that strange things are afoot at the old railroad overpass. It just may be that it isn't Lydia. Or that Lydia was made up to explain the weird events.

One favorite part of the legend, not often told, and one that has also been part of other tales similar to this is included in the story here. Our hero gives Lydia his sweater to keep her warm from the chilled air. After approaching the mother, he can't believe Lydia was a ghost. The mother insists, and tells the young local where she is buried. The next day he goes to the cemetery. He finds her grave, and upon it, neatly folded, is his sweater that he gave her the night before.

No, really!

Gold Hill....

Gold Hill, if any town can be haunted, is likely to have ghostly spirits wandering the land. The tales told here only scratch the surface of what spirits walk the area. The legends seem to embrace the idea of men who came to dig, to make the money that only a gold mine can offer, only to lose their lives in a cave in, a fight, a disease or illness, and then their spirits walk the land, cursed and cursing the people who placed a value on the gold they dug that was higher than the value of human life. Gold Hill not only offers a book on all the ghosts that may be in the town, but also has a very popular ghost walk at the end of July every year. The tours are filled with hundreds of interested ghost hunters, amateur and professional, who often wait hours for their turn to take a tour of the town late at night. Paranormal investigators have been welcomed to visit, as well, at other times. While the town now is quaint, a glossy reproduction of a hard life village of the past, the place still was a mine, and even though the shafts may be empty of everything except ghosts, they have been known to collapse on occasion. The town and area is hollow. It's impossible to know whether or not the place one person treads is safer than any other. Don't end up the next ghost on the list in Gold Hill!

Founders Hall...

Legends like this often exist in multiple settings. Duke University also makes this claim, and with the school having a medical campus, one could see how a tale of a stolen corpse would get attached to the university, though it would have to have been Trinity College at the time.

The legend may have actually come from both some urban legends and some made up tales at the closer by Davidson College. The old Chambers building was part of the North Carolina Medical College and classes were held there until it moved to Charlotte. Rumors of ghosts, including Louise, and stolen cadavers buried in mass graves were part of the lore. There even was a tale that the columns of the original Chambers Building, which burned to the ground, leaving only the two columns standing, were filled with old body parts from dissection. The tale is highly improbable, considering the difficulty of depositing the bodies, the need to hide the evidence, and the smell it would make.

Sally's Bridge...

As with many of these urban legends, there is little reality to the story and haunting. Whispered incantations will probably not bring back the ghosts of the dead here. Even the tale is full of inconsistencies that often occur with this type of story. Sally was going to the prom in some tales in the 1950s, some in the 1970s. While boys were certainly creeps in both eras, it would seem odd for her to drive to her date's house, have him stand her up, and then her drive home. Wouldn't he have gone to her place? Or not, as the story seems to imply?

However, the bridge and area seem to give off a creepy vibe, most likely just because it is out in the middle of nowhere on a dangerous road. Some people have reported seeing orbs and getting vague ominous feelings at the bridge.

There is another Sally's Bridge, in Concord, with a slightly similar tale, and the two often get their legends mixed up.

Lake Lure Inn & Spa...

It could be that the Inn & Spa just *seems* haunted. It really gives off the haunted vibe with its old look, the windows glowing at night, the quietude, the dark evenings with good places for ghosts to hide. Some of the legends that have been attached may be more hyperbole than fact. Ghosts in the inn have even been attributed as being the spirits of Grover Cleveland or Franklin Roosevelt. When Patrick Swayze, star of *Dirty Dancing*, passed, it was soon speculated that he might also haunt the Inn.

While the inn itself doesn't put forth some of the rumors, it certainly doesn't hurt to have this natural or unnatural promotion for its business. A more recent photo of a ghostly man or boy made the rounds in recent times, showing the ghostly image in the restaurant. This was as likely to be form of pareidolia, where a viewer sees something recognizable in an image of mixed items.

So while the inn may or may not be actually haunted, one thing is for sure, it's in a nice location to vacation. Don't worry about ghosts and just go.

Lodge on Lake Lure...

Honestly, walking through the Lodge on Lake Lure late at night is a bit creepy. It's just so quiet in there, and the windows open up to complete darkness on the outside. It's hard to use a *feeling* to say a place is haunted, but, well, this place kind of has it.

Curiously, the idea that it is George Penn that haunts the place doesn't really seem to fit with the history. Penn died in a shootout with criminals who had stolen meat in a truck. They ran past a roadside scale, and when Penn chased them down, they began to shoot at him. Returning fire, Penn was gunned down by the two crooks when he finally ran out of ammunition. He died in Fairview, near the Swannanoa weigh station. Only after his death was the Lodge founded and dedicated to him.

An alternate identity of the ghost, and one that seems to make more sense, is that it is Jesse A. Sullins, a former highway patrolman and a caretaker for the Lodge when it was still a retreat for the officers. The Lodge was used up until the 1960s, when the town of Lake Lure bought the Lodge and it was sold to a number of different owners. The ghost never seemed to appear until the 1980s, and more often once it was turned into an inn for the public. Sullins was disappointed that the old retreat was no longer in use for officers. He died in 1981. It would seem that if there was a ghost, and that ghost had some reason to stick around, it would more likely be the ghost of Sullins, who actually spent time there, rather than the spirit of someone who was never there, when the building didn't even exist in his lifetime, and he would know nothing about it.

So, next time someone stays there, and they need toilet paper, ask for Jesse. See what happens.

Helen's Bridge...

Helen's Bridge has benefitted from a bit of natural and unnatural consequences. The old stone bridge, high up over the road, hidden in the mountains and far away from daily life, gives it an otherworldly appearance. The bridge hangs over the gap as if separating one plane of existence from another. In addition, while the tales of seeing Helen may be apocryphal, the area has become a hotspot for paranormal investigations, and just the idea that there could be something there adds to the story.

On the other side, there really is no Helen. Many people have tied in a Helen to this and other stories. There just was no event that led up to this haunting. John Evans Brown lost two sons, and his first wife, while in Australia, and died before the bridge was ever built. Philip Henry lost his wife, Florine, to a fire in New York, before he moved to Asheville. The property was owned by his two daughters until 1961. There was no report of a fire in the stables, usually the root cause of the death of Helen's daughter. The original part of the house, built by Brown, was torn down on purpose, but this, too, was not connected with the stables or the bridge. There may be something out there on the bridge, but most likely, Helen is just a story made up to scare people on a late night out.

Riverside Cemetery...

So, even though there are lots of famous people buried there, the only ghosts are Confederate soldiers that march in a regiment through the cemetery, so the story goes. The battle, such as it was, did happen. Union troops retreating into Tennessee were told that Asheville could be attacked and taken only if there was a guarantee of little loss on their side. A small group of Union troops advanced on the city, which was home to Confederate soldiers being mustered in and through the

Army. When a group of 1000 Union troops attacked the city, 300 militia were rounded up to defend their home from entrenched earthworks. They easily drove the Union back. The battle itself took place along the property of nearby UNC-Asheville more than the cemetery.

Unfortunately, a group of very living ghouls decided to do their own reenactment. Some people were dressing up as zombies and wandering the cemetery at night. Just another reason not to go there after dark.

Biltmore...

For the longest time, employees were instructed not to talk about the ghosts. It may come from a time when it was thought that ghost stories would scare away more people than they brought. The legends are well known now.

The ghosts aren't seen easily, as said in the main chapter. While the legends pass on, there really haven't been any reports from visitors in a long time, and no photos of the ghosts have shown up. That could be because the ghosts are more heard than seen. Only George is occasionally said to appear in the library, as a shadow. And that usually is tied in with an approaching storm. George was known to happily ride his lands, at one with the forest, until he spied a thunderstorm on the horizon. Once the storm approached, he would excuse himself to the solitude of the library.

The tales of George, Edith, the mysterious Weeping Lady, all seem to hint at less of a ghostly haunt, and more residual events that happened so frequently or were so important that they imparted some sort of permanent embossing upon the place. Instead of witnessing ghosts, they could be the events of past lives being seen. It could explain why they are more likely seen by the employees, or only seen at certain times of the day.

One other haunted area, normally never mentioned, is the spiral staircase that leads to the tower. Guests have reported feeling someone push them, an invisible spirit pushing them out of the way as they slowly trudge up the steps.

Cowee Tunnel...

If any place would be haunted by tragedy, this would be it. The sad tale doesn't even come close to describing the actual horror of these events, or even the day to day life of prisoners ripped from their families and homes for either petty crimes or in most cases no reason at all other than to feed the need for free labor. The prisoners were simply rented out for up to a year from the prison system to private companies, with little to no accountability.

The bodies of the prisoners who lost their lives in the river were not buried on the mountain, as the legend tells. It makes the story sound better to think that the graves hold the spirits of the men, and their tears trickle into the cave. However, the actual event happened to the east of the tunnel, and the mountain would be a poor and difficult place to bury the dead. They were actually hauled up to the nearest flat piece of land and buried in probably three mass graves, in a spot near what is now Jackson County Green Energy Park.

For a less realistic tragedy, yet one that has some similarity, the railroad was used to film a train wreck scene for the movie *The Fugitive*. In it, falsely accused Richard Kimble is involved in a bus wreck that sends the bus tumbling onto a train track. The other inmates flee, but Kimble stays to help a guard escape an oncoming train that crashes into the bus. The old bus and train carcass can be seen on the trip by the Great Smoky Mountain Railroad.

Locations

All locations given are approximate, though as always I have tried to be as exact as possible. There may be errors, or certain things may have gotten moved or destroyed. This book is presented as entertainment. The safety of travel and arrival at any location cannot be guaranteed by the author. Always check for safety and legal access before going to any of these places. Some legends have no distinct location, and as such there is no exact place to visit, so a viable estimate was given.

Many of these places are private or restricted. Do not enter or even go on the property of any of them without permission. Even several public locations require a fee to visit. Be respectful of others' property.

The GPS coordinates include a minus sign, (-), for the longitude. Be sure to include this or use the N and W distinctions when putting the coordinates in any mapping tool or GPS unit.

Acknowledgements

As always, thanks go out to several people who helped with this endeavor. I got to talk with lots of paranormal investigators throughout this, and they were all supportive of my writing the book, even with my skeptic bent. Eddie and Jeffrey from NC HAGS, Stanley Wardrip down in Wilmington from Carolina's Unknown, Michael La Chiana from the Heritage Hunters Society. I had lots of good, but quiet, contacts with public places that may not want their names out there, but you know who you are! Thanks for believing and sharing your stories. Big thanks and love to my wife for her support (though why she lets me do this I'll never know), and my family, especially my brother John for telling all those spooky stories. That's for another book.

Photography Credits

I took time to write this book, but allowed for more leniencies in the photography. Not every spooky tree or haunted bridge needed to be photographed for this book. I am indebted to the people who either supplied me with photos of their travels, or in other cases have placed images into Creative Commons, a licensing that allows for reuse of photos with proper credit. Their inclusion does not represent an endorsement of the work or ideas within. Reproduction of any images or text without permission is prohibited unless granted by the owner. All photos by the author unless otherwise noted.

Nags Head Woods –Chris Updegrave

Fort Macon – John B. Sledge, Jr.

Cotton Exchange – Edward Orde (CC)

St. James Episcopal Church – Edward Orde (CC)

Bellamy Mansion – James Woodward (CC)

Thalian Hall – Benjamin Thompson (CC)

Fort Fisher – Public Domain

Captain Charlie's – John Sledge III

Bentonville Battlefield – Erin Rebecca (CC)

Cryptozoology and Paranormal Museum – Stephen Barcelo

Mordecai House – Public Domain

Oakwood Cemetery – 2BKNIGHT (CC)

Gimghoul Castle – Michelle Sledge

Grandfather Mountain – Public Domain

Grove Park Inn – Selena NBH (CC)

Helen's Bridge – Molly Hare (CC)

Green Mountain Inn -Michael La Chiana, The Heritage Hunters Society

Hot Springs – Stacy Harris-Radford

Items marked with a (CC) are linked to permission given in Creative Commons, an allowance to use certain photos under certain conditions. All photos used under (CC) allow for reuse, with modifications, for commercial purposes, as long as proper credit is given. I endeavored to find the real names of any photographer if possible, and gave credit under what names I had or were supplied. A link to the Creative Commons page can be found here...

creativecommons.org/licenses/by-sa/4.0/deed.en

About the Author

Joe Sledge is a North Carolina native and a graduate of the University of North Carolina at Chapel Hill, where he developed a love for exploring. He grew up on the Outer Banks where he spent all summers with sand between his toes, and the rest of the year waiting to get his toes in the sand. Joe worked for nine years as a special education teacher before writing his first book, *Did You See That? A GPS Guide to North Carolina's Out of the Ordinary Attractions*. He is very happily married and has a quite wonderful daughter, who gets most of his time and attention when he's not writing, and even when he is.

Made in the USA
Middletown, DE
19 May 2022

65968197R00144